The
GARBAGE MAN
Always Comes
on FRIDAYS

12 Steps for
Improving Your
Relationship
with God

The GARBAGE MAN Always Comes on FRIDAYS

12 Steps for Improving Your Relationship with God

Rev.

Kristine A. Belfils

Copyright © 2005 Kris Belfils Ministries

"Brokenness," p. 52, from Brokenness CD, Copyright © 2002 Kristine A. Belfils
"I Am Free," p. 55, from Brokenness CD, Copyright © 2002 Kristine A. Belfils
"Cross of Grace," p. 69, from Brokenness CD, Copyright © 2002 Kristine A. Belfils
"Listen and Obey," p. 79, from Brokenness CD, Copyright © 2002 Kristine A. Belfils
"My Defense," p. 99, from Brokenness CD, Copyright © 2002 Kristine A. Belfils
"Secret Place," p. 103, from Brokenness CD, Copyright © 2002 Kristine A. Belfils
"My Rock and My Song," p. 134 from Brokenness CD,
Copyright © 2002 Kristine A. Belfils

Rev. Kristine A. Belfils
Phone: 509-994-1965
E-mail: Kris@KrisBelfils.com
www.KrisBelfils.com

Library of Congress Cataloging-in-Publication Data

Belfils, Kristine A., 1964-
The garbage man always comes on Fridays : 12 steps
for improving your relationship with God / Kristine A. Belfils.
p. cm.
Includes bibliographical references.
ISBN 1451513100 (pbk. : alk. paper)
1. Spiritual life--Christianity. 2. Christian life. I. Title.

DEDICATION

To my beautiful family.
Your love, encouragement, and support
have helped me write this book.

CONTENTS

                Quick, Joyful, and Total

Chapter 10:   Step Eight: Finding Encouragement, 80
                Help from the Psalms

Chapter 11:   Step Nine: Learning How to Trust God, 93
                Trust Factor

Chapter 12:   Step Ten: Surviving Life in the Mundane, 100
                Endurance and the Secret Place

Chapter 13:   Step Eleven: Receiving God's Discipline, 106
                Don't Fight the Correction of God

Chapter 14:   Step Twelve: God of the Second Chance, 117
                Hope for Ministry Again

Chapter 15:   I Saved Your Tricycle! 135
                A Father and Daughter Reunited

Chapter 16:   The Garbage Man Always Comes on Fridays! 139
                A New Beginning!

                Bible Translations, 144
                Endnotes, 145

ACKNOWLEDGMENTS

As I think of the process of healing I went through, there are many to thank who helped aid in my complete restoration.

First, I thank my Heavenly Father for Your Fatherly love. You have healed and transformed my life into something beautiful. Holy Spirit, thank you for being my Counselor, Comforter, and Friend. You were there in the lonely times. You spoke to my spirit in so many ways. Thank You my Lord and Savior Jesus Christ for Your mercy and grace. Thank you for Your robe of righteousness you have given me by your sacrifice for my sins on the cross. Your robe covers all of me and I am forever beautiful.

I thank my Husband, Ron, for your unconditional love and encouragement. Ron, after we came home from my attempted suicide, you helped heal my wounds. You spoke life to me. I saw God's strength in you to help me stand. Then you were my spiritual crutches under my arms to help me walk. Eventually I walked on my own again. Your life is an example to me of Christ's love. May I be the wife, lover, and friend you need and deserve.

Thank you to my loving daughters, Tori and Karissa. You were very young when this season happened in your mother's life. Your little giggles and precious smiles were strength to me. Mommy needed your love and that is what you gave me. You didn't know anything different. I am sorry for trying to end my life. It was a selfish act. I am thankful to be alive, and also very thankful to see you both grow up. Please remember our choices have consequences. My choices were not good. My prayer is that you will never make the same mistakes I did. I pray that through this book, you and others will understand how important it is to stay close to Jesus. It is extremely important to stay humble and broken before God. Remember to trust Jesus always and to not rely on your own understanding (Proverbs 3:5 & 6). This is what I have learned through this process.

I would like to thank all those that had a hand in helping me heal and walk out of my failure. Ron Moreland (my brother and friend), Pastor Don and Julie Stevens, Pastor Russ and Jennifer Tappero, and the many pastors that helped me in my recovery; Pastor Russ and Cindy Doyl, for a new beginning; and my friend, Cherie Millsap, who didn't judge but only supported. Some of you were part of the refining fire season and some of you were God's love in the flesh.

PREFACE

Before I begin ...

I write these words with much prayer and trembling! It would be easier to write a book about a certain Bible topic and show you how to apply it to your life than it is to write this book. I am making myself vulnerable to you, the reader, for I will share my life, my actions, my emotions, my reactions to my sin, and how I overcame by the power of Jesus Christ. I write this because it helps me heal, and I pray that it ministers to you.

Please don't look at my life as an example of purity and holiness, because you will not find such an example. I'm only a sinner saved by grace, but there are truths I've found that have set me free from bondage and self-destruction. Please focus on the truths. I write this book not to glorify my sin, but to help those who might have fallen, as I did. The apostle Paul wrote in II Corinthians 1:3 & 4 (NKJV); *"Blessed be the God and Father of our Lord Jesus Christ, the Father of mercies and God of all comfort, who comforts us in all our tribulation, that we may be able to comfort those who are in any trouble, with the comfort with which we ourselves are comforted by God."* May the words in this book comfort those who need comfort and encourage those who need encouragement.

Also, it is my hope that those who've been hurt by a fallen minister will see the other side, the side of the one who has failed. May they find healing, and perhaps, show mercy and grace to the fallen minister. Aside from the above, you can also look at this book as "Christianity 101." Maybe you've never failed, or someone has never failed you; still there are basic helps for your everyday life of faith to help you stay close to Christ and grow in His love.

God has brought me through a horrific time in my life and has given me hope to keep living. Not only to keep living, but to have more abundant life than I've ever thought possible. The Garbage Man Always Comes On Fridays is a personal account of my walk out of failure and into a new beginning, a second chance for life, family, and ministry. To understand the title of this book, you need to read the entire book through the last chapter. You will find there why it is entitled; The Garbage Man Always Comes on Fridays.

Christ died for us all, no matter what we've done, He died so that we might live. To quote words from a song I wrote right after my failure, "There is a Hope! There is a cross! There was a sacrifice for our shame! He gave his life! He took our place! We can hide behind the Cross of Grace,"[1] and hold our heads up high as we finish this race and ultimately spend eternity with our Savior, Jesus Christ our Lord.

I pray the words in this book will minister to you the reader, and my prayer is:

"God, if someone who is reading this has gone or is going through something similar to what I've been through, please wrap Your unconditional loving arms around them and carry them through this process. You have a plan for their life and You will never turn from that plan. Thank You for the hope this brings to our hearts. We love You Lord, and we totally give our lives to You. Have Your way in us. Amen."

In Christ's forgiven love,
Kris Belfils

Chapter 1

THE STORY

Ambulance and ER

Sirens blared from the ambulance as it sped through the streets of Airway Heights, Washington, near Spokane.

Inside the ambulance, Mike, the EMT, checked my vital signs. I had deliberately taken an overdose of sleeping pills to try to stop the madness in my mind. Whenever I would sleep I didn't have to think about the mess I was in. If only I could just sleep forever and never wake up! Yet I was made to sit up in the ambulance in an effort to keep me from falling asleep.

"Why'd you do this?" Mike asked. "Why did you want to hurt yourself?"

"Christian?" I mumbled.

"Yes," he replied.

I tried to tell him all the wrong choices I'd made in the past year -- how I'd hurt my husband, how I'd lost my job as a pastor. But as I was talking I could tell Mike didn't understand what I was saying. The sleeping pills were impairing my speech. The more I tried to talk to Mike, the faster he worked on me. He knocked on the window to the cab of the ambulance to get the driver's attention. "Hurry up," he shouted. "We're losing her!" The engine raced louder and faster.

How had I come to this place in my life? Would my life end? At this point, I didn't care. I only wanted to stop hurting my husband and family. I couldn't fix or change what I had done and I felt my life was out of control. All of this never should've happened. After all, I was a strong woman. I always landed on my feet when troubles came. You could always rely on me for help and acceptance. Now, the one who gave help desperately needed it, yet I would never admit it.

As I sat on the gurney, I looked through the ambulance's rear windows. Tears welled up in my eyes. If only I could turn back the time, if only I'd made different choices. Why was I going through all of this? I never thought I would try to kill myself.

"I'm sorry, honey," I whispered, as I strained to see my husband driving behind the ambulance. He wasn't there. "This all must be a nightmare," I thought.

The ambulance arrived at the hospital and I was rushed to the emergency room. Vaguely, a shout penetrated my foggy mind. "She's fading fast! Not much time before she stops responding!"

I found myself in the emergency room wearing a hospital gown. People were talking to me from all directions. I tried to answer them but it was as if I spoke a foreign language. They would just look at me as if I spoke something crazy. There were so many voices yelling at me while the room was spinning. My ears seemed plugged up. Nobody made any sense to me. What was wrong with these people? One by one I tried to answer all the voices. Why don't they listen to me?

Nurse Thompson looked at me and asked the same question over and over: "Did you take anything else? Did you just take the sleeping pills or was there anything else?" The room continued to spin and everyone and everything seemed so far away from me. I tried to reply, "No, that's all," but the nurse didn't understand. Where was Ron? I was determined to find him. I kept looking all over the room and at every face that came into view, but I didn't see him.

Two men entered and slowly walked up to my bed. I could barely tell it was my former pastor and a board member from the church I had to resign from. "What were they doing here?" I thought. I was so tired. Wasn't it enough I wasn't a pastor at their church anymore? It was as if salt was being poured all over my deep bleeding wound. It stung! Embarrassment and shame filled my heart. "Why don't they leave?" I thought. They stood at the foot of my bed. Tears came to my eyes again as I asked my pastor, "Please forgive me. I am sorry."

"I forgive you," Pastor Smith said.

Regret and pain overwhelmed me; how can I forgive myself?

I felt myself slipping into a dream. In the dream I recognized people from my past. Friends, mentors, and family members, I wanted to talk to them all. One by one I would ask them to forgive me. Quickly the doctor asked the visitors to leave. A nurse rushed over to me. "Wake up! Wake up, Kris!" she shouted! She made me sit up in bed to make it harder for me to fall asleep. They gave me a cup of thick, black gunk to drink, while another nurse encouraged me to drink it all. It was gross. But by this time, I wanted to live. I would do anything to help myself now. Faced with death, I realized this was not where I wanted to go. After drinking down the black stuff I felt sick to my stomach. I needed to throw up. The nurses encouraged me to try. I threw up a little, but it was not enough. The nurse gave me another cup of the thick, black, charcoal drink. Again, I drank, and again the two nurses shouted: "Drink, keep drinking, all of it!" I felt ill. I tried to throw up, but couldn't. I could hardly hold myself up. All I wanted to do was sleep.

Nurse Thompson came to the front of me. "Open up, I need to look inside your mouth," she insisted. As I opened my mouth another nurse took my hands and held them behind my back. A tube was pushed deeper and deeper into the back of my throat.

"What are they doing to me?" I thought. I tried to get my hands free so I could pull the tube out of my throat. A nurse said, "Because you didn't throw up the charcoal drink, this is the only way to try and get rid of all the pills you took. We are trying to pump your stomach." Again I tried to stop them but couldn't move my arms and hands. The tube hurt my throat. I started to gag and began to throw up more and more. I was out of control again. No one understood me.

Finally Thompson said, "Good! That's it, good job," and the tube was taken out of my mouth.

The doctor walked in my room. "You'll have to stay awake for awhile. You did throw up some of the pills, but, a good portion of them has already dissolved in your system."

The two visitors came back into my room. They commented on my new black lipstick I was wearing. What were they talking about? I didn't realize the black drink I had to take now stained my lips.

I wanted to live! If I died, I would lose out on my life with my husband and children and the enemy of my soul would win. Now, I was determined to stay awake. Pastor Smith and Don, the board member, stayed by my side. I asked them to talk to me and keep me awake. I tried to answer their questions and keep in the conversation but they were far away in my mind. Every once in a while I would just stop talking and look at them. They started to laugh. I must not have made sense again.

Finally Ron came into my room. He rushed up to me and told me he loved me.

"I'm sorry for everything!" I cried. Did he understand? Did he realize how much I really did love him? "Am I going to die?" I asked. He didn't answer. I asked again, and again he didn't respond. He must not have understood or possibly, I thought, it was too late and I was going to die but he didn't want to tell me that. Again, I tried. He looked up at the monitors, then held my face in his hands, "No, you're not going to die!" he whispered. "You're going to live."

During my time in the emergency room, I saw Jesus. He wore white robes and looked at me and smiled. I told Ron, "Jesus was in the room," but he didn't understand me. At that moment, when Jesus was there, I could think clearly. I knew Jesus loved me no matter what I've done and he would be with me always. He would be there to help me walk on with life. He would be with me to help heal and restore my relationship with Ron. He would be with my husband to heal his wounds. Jesus was with me in that room and such peace filled my heart. I knew I was going to live.

Day turned to night and the doctor told me I could go to sleep. It was hard because I'd just spent the last nine hours trying to stay awake. The scenes of the day raced around in my head. Was it all a dream? Would I wake up and find out it never happened? This had to be a nightmare!

As I opened my eyes to face the morning light, I realized it was not a dream. It all happened: my failure, my anger, the loss of my job, and yesterday, trying to kill myself. How would I walk on? How could I live after what I had done? So many mistakes, and so many bad choices. How could my husband love me again, let alone forgive me?

Chapter 2

A FORGIVING HUSBAND

Loving as Christ Loves the Church

Ron and I were married June 22, 1985. We've had ups and downs in our marriage, but there has come a place in us where we can now be ourselves and truly love each other for who we are, as individuals and as a couple. We have finally trusted God to mold each other instead of each of us trying to make the other change. I can say that today because of the transforming power of God, and the brokenness and humility Ron and I both experienced.

Ron forgave me from the very beginning of my confession to him. I don't understand his forgiveness or love for me, but I'm extremely grateful. I asked him one day, "Why didn't you cast me out and have no part of me?" His response was overwhelming. "I'm supposed to love you as Christ loves the Church. How does Christ love the church? He forgives, protects, and cherishes His bride."

Had I heard him correctly? Did he say that he loves me as Christ loves the Church? I've always known Christ's forgiving love and power, but now I was seeing it firsthand through my husband. The love of Christ has always overwhelmed me. Now the love from my husband was almost unreal. I was always expecting Ron to change his mind, especially as we walked together through the months that followed. Ron was a rock; an unmovable, solid, unshakable rock. I never saw those character traits in him before. God showed me how precious a husband I have in Ron.

Before this failure, Ron and I were struggling in our marriage.

Looking back, I see our relationship as many years of me wanting to have my way, and Ron not knowing what to do with me. I grew up without a father figure in my life. I learned to cope and do a lot of things on my own. From putting together an entertainment center, changing the oil of my car, or making decisions by myself as opposed to asking my dad for advice, I really had no need to submit to a male authority. When I married Ron, things stayed the same. I didn't understand the principle of submission to my husband and he never pushed the issue. In the beginning, he seemed to enjoy my strong will and drive. As the years progressed, however, my independence took a toll on our marriage and relationship.

Ron grew up playing a passive role in a fairly strict home. He usually kept to himself and stayed in his room. He responded similarly with me in our marriage and became passive about decisions. "Whatever you want is all right with me," he would always tell me. This was frustrating because there came a time in my heart when I wanted to submit. I wanted Ron to be a man. He was afraid to make a mistake. His insecurities caused him to be sarcastic and harsh to me. This created a distance between us. I would ask him, "What's wrong?" He'd realize the problem and it would be all right for a few months and then he'd act the same way again, which dug into my heart. He'd be withdrawn, almost depressed at times. Our acquaintances didn't pick up on this pattern but those who were close to me did. They saw how he acted and questioned it. At first I did anything to try to help him. Things would be better for a few months, then it would happen again. I grew to resent him and his treatment of me.

God worked on his heart and brought Ron to a place of brokenness. He finally asked for help. He went to a pastor who was a friend of ours, for advice and encouragement.

Ron picked up a book at a Christian bookstore, *The Power of A Praying Husband*,[2] by Stormie Omartian, and began to read it. He would tell me things from the book and prayed for me openly. I started to see a change in him. He began to treat me better. I thought it would be like before and he'd go back to his old ways of treating me, so I didn't believe the change would stay. It did. God brought Ron to a place of needing Him. Ron encouraged me to read the book, *The Power of A Praying Wife*.[3] I did! It helped me to pray specifically for Ron in areas

I hadn't even thought about. I have to say these two books were a part of our marriage restoration.

Praying for each other is huge. We pray together in the morning before Ron goes to work and we pray in the evening together before we go to sleep. During the day we may call each other, and if one of us is in need of prayer, we pray for the other. We have seen God answer our prayers over and over. From emotions being healed, to wisdom with our daughters, to finances and things of our home, God has directed us through answered prayers. I can truthfully say our marriage is better than it ever was. Ron and I have found each other. We respect each other and cherish and guard our relationship daily. We both feel this is the biggest miracle that has come out of this whole journey in our lives...a transformed marriage.

Chapter 3

STEP I: CHOOSE
TO BELIEVE THE TRUTH

Lies, Lies, All lies

It took some time for me to realize that the way I was thinking about myself was not healthy. I could encourage anyone on earth, but when it came to me, my thoughts were mostly negative and self-destructive. There were many sources for my negative self-image. Much of it started when I was younger, long before my failure. The teasing of childish friends or an adult, who spoke down to me, could have easily contributed. I'm sure many incidences affected my poor self-image, yet at the time of my failure, all I saw was the doom and gloom of my immediate bad choices.

To overcome one's negative thoughts about one's self is a hard task, indeed. Many years have built the foundation of how you think about yourself today. If you have thoughts of worthlessness or feel you're a loser, please realize there are several sources for those lies. Here are two major contributors:

1. THE ENEMY WILL SPEAK LIES TO YOU

Satan wants to destroy us all! What better way than to use ourselves against us? He will speak lies to you about yourself to get you to self-destruct. He will speak lies to you about your future. He will speak lies about anything and everything concerning us. Here are a few verses that show his character.

John 10:10 (Amplified Bible)
"The thief comes only in order to steal and kill and destroy. I came that they may have and enjoy life, and have it in abundance (to the full, till it overflows)."

John 8:44 (Amplified Bible)
"...he (the Devil) was a murderer from the beginning and does not stand in the truth, because there is no truth in him. When he speaks a falsehood, he speaks what is natural to him, for he is a liar [himself] and the father of lies and of all that is false."

"...of all that is false." That's the Devil's character. He constantly tells us falsehoods about ourselves. If we are not careful, we will listen to those lies and act upon them. The enemy will fill your mind with feelings of worthlessness about yourself to destroy you. He'll fill your mind with negative thoughts about you, your family and friends, and everything else you come in contact with. Thoughts like, "There's no good in me." "Why did I do that? How stupid can I be?" "No one cares about me or what I do."

Please, if this is you, STOP listening to false information. It's not true. God has a hope and a future for each one of us. Fill your mind with truth about your future!

Jeremiah 29:11 (Amplified Bible)
"For I know the thoughts and plans that I have for you, says the Lord, thoughts and plans for welfare and peace and not for evil, to give you hope in your final outcome."

When you think you don't have a future or your life seems hopeless, think again! Hold on to the promise that God has a plan and that it is a good one for your life. He has planned this for you from the beginning of time. He created you for that plan! In spite of your failure, in spite of the lies that you are listening to, God will use you again. The key to following God's plan is to trust Him and obey what He asks. I will address obeying God in a later chapter, but just touch on this for a second, we have to do our part for God's hope and future to come about in our lives. Our part is obedience. Our part is to trust God. God's word is filled with guidelines for our lives that we must obey. Also, listen to that still, small voice as God speaks to your heart. Listen and obey! Even in the small things. This will help us keep our thoughts and actions in check.

2. YOU CAN SPEAK LIES TO YOURSELF

We can tell ourselves the worst result will happen and inevitably will because of our negative attitude. We can lie to ourselves about how good we are and how bad our neighbor is. We can listen to ourselves instead of God's word and make bad choices for our lives. We can sabotage our future. Here are a few scriptures to show this.

Proverbs 23:7a (Amplified Bible)
"For as he thinks in his heart, so is he..."

Jeremiah 17:9 (Amplified Bible)
"The heart is deceitful above all things, and it is exceedingly perverse and corrupt and severely, mortally sick! Who can know it [perceive, understand, be acquainted with his own heart and mind]?"

Mark 7:21-23 (Amplified Bible)
"For from within, [that is] out of the hearts of men, come base and wicked thoughts, sexual immorality, stealing, murder, adultery, coveting (a greedy desire to have more wealth), dangerous and destructive wickedness, deceit; unrestrained (indecent) conduct; an evil eye (envy), slander (evil speaking, malicious misrepresentation, abusiveness), pride (the sin of an uplifted heart against God and man), foolishness (folly, lack of sense, recklessness, thoughtlessness). All these evil [purposes and desires] come from within, and they make the man unclean and render him unhallowed.

Ephesians 4:22-25 (Amplified Bible)

"Strip yourselves of your former nature [put off and discard your old unrenewed self] which characterized your previous manner of life and becomes corrupt through lusts and desires that spring from delusion; And be constantly renewed in the spirit of your mind [having a fresh mental and spiritual attitude], And put on the new nature (the regenerate self) created in God's image, [Godlike] in true righteousness and holiness. Therefore, rejecting all falsity and being done now with it, let everyone express the truth with his neighbor, for we are all parts of one body and members one of another.)"

"...rejecting all falsity and being done now with it," is what we have to do when we recognize a lie we believe about our self. If it does not line up with what the word of God says you are, reject it immediately, even when you've been in the habit of saying it to yourself over and over again. The only one who can stop lying to you about yourself is you!

It's hard to know the difference between a lie about yourself and something that's possibly true, that you can change. Yet, there's a harshness the Devil uses that is usually direct and painful. Thoughts that bring doom and gloom, that bring no hope, are the key to knowing a lie. When negative thoughts come into your mind, if you dwell on them for any length of time, they begin to take root in your heart. They start becoming your paradigm, or how you look at life. This is when it becomes unhealthy. As you dwell on how bad you are, you'll begin to believe it and start to act or react out of that unhealthy outlook.

CHOOSE TO BELIEVE TRUTH

The only thing that would combat this in my life was truth from the word of God--what it says about me and who I am in Christ. I've read a lot of books during my journey out of failure. The book that best helped me to realize who I was in Christ in spite of what I'd done, was *The Search for Significance*, by Robert S. McGee.[4] I would recommend this book to anyone. In it there are truths found in scripture we can apply to our lives. I added the Amplified Bible version after each truth from his book.

1. I'm Deeply Loved

I John 4:9 & 10 (Amplified Bible)
"In this the love of God was made manifest (displayed) where we are concerned: in that God sent His Son, the only begotten or unique [Son], into the world so that we might live through Him. In this is love: not that we loved God, but that He loved us and sent His Son to be the propitiation (the atoning sacrifice) for our sins."

2. I Am Completely Forgiven

Romans 5:1 (Amplified Bible)
"Therefore since we are justified (acquitted, declared righteous, and given a right standing with God) through faith, let us [grasp the fact that we] have [the peace of reconciliation to hold and to enjoy] peace with God through our Lord Jesus Christ (the Messiah, the Anointed One)."

3. I Am Totally Accepted by God

Colossians 1:21 & 22 (Amplified Bible)
"And although you at one time were estranged and alienated from Him and were of hostile attitude of mind in your wicked activities, Yet now has [Christ, the Messiah] reconciled [you to God] in the body of His flesh through death, in order to present you holy and faultless and irreproachable in His [the Father's] presence."

4. I'm a New Creation and Complete in Christ

II Corinthians 5:17 (Amplified Bible)
"Therefore if any person is [ingrafted] in Christ (the Messiah) he is a new creation (a new creature altogether); the old [previous moral and spiritual condition] has passed away. Behold, the fresh and new has come."

I finally received these truths in my spirit. What really helped me to remember and believe them was to print them out and place them around my house. I encourage you to do what it takes to remember and believe them too.

These truths helped me to walk on. It took some time for me to believe them because I was a pastor who knew right from wrong, and I failed. Surely it was meant for the unbeliever who didn't know Christ. That was a lie from the enemy I was tripping over time and again. But, these truths are for me and for you! No matter if we have just become a believer or if we've followed Christ our entire lives and then fail, sin is sin. God doesn't rate sin; only people do.

If these scriptures didn't apply to me, then Christ died in vain. Realizing this made me accept them as my own and walk in them. I'm a new creature. My past is forgiven, the old is passed away, and all things are fresh and new. I also found a scripture in my daily study, which goes along with these passages I've just shared.

Philippians 3:13 & 14 (NKJV)

"Brethren, I do not count myself to have apprehended; but one thing I do, forgetting those things which are behind and reaching forward to those things which are ahead. I press toward the goal for the prize of the upward call of God in Christ Jesus."

Paul said to forget what's behind. To not remember it any longer! To reach forward to those things which are ahead! Our past is in our past. We can and will press onward to "...the goal for the prize of the upward call of God...." Praise God for His forgiveness and power to help us walk on without shame! The enemy will try to lie to you, tell you your future is ruined, you will never be able to minister again, let alone walk on from your mistake. Don't listen to that lie! God tells us to press on, walk on, to that "upward call of God" in your life. What the Devil meant for harm, God will use for good!

It is interesting and true; "Satan lies to unbelievers to convince them they're not guilty while he lies to believers to convince them they are guilty."[5] Have you found yourself, as a believer, feeling guilty or condemned? There's a huge difference between condemnation and conviction. "Conviction is meant to lift us out of something, to help us move up higher in God's will and plan for our lives. Condemnation presses us down and puts us under a burden of guilt."[6] It is healthy and normal to feel guilty when we are initially convicted of sin; but to keep the guilty feeling after we've repented of the sin is not healthy, nor is it God's will.

Conviction from the Lord never fills us with condemning shame. Shame fills us with a painful sense of disgrace and heavy, humiliating regret, which leaves us feeling hopeless. We can fall under the weight of regret if we're not careful. It's very heavy and seems to come up often as we walk out of failure. We cannot change the past. We cannot change our choices or previous actions, but God can and does bring hope in the midst of dealing with the bad choices.

I thought God would wipe out all the consequences of my sin once I asked forgiveness, but he didn't. I will talk more about the consequences I had to go through in the next chapter. I thought God would take care of anything that would be hard for me to endure. But, the very walking through the consequences of my actions made me stronger. It made me learn to trust and obey God each step of the way.

There are some positive answers for those negative thoughts that might enter our minds. You might think no one really loves or cares about you.

John 3:16 (Amplified Bible)

"For God so greatly loved and dearly prized the world that He [even] gave up His only begotten (unique) Son, so that whoever believes in (trusts in, clings to, relies on) Him shall not perish (come to destruction, be lost) but have eternal (everlasting) life."

We are loved and dearly prized, each one of us. God loved us so much that He gave His only Son to us. This is a gift from God. Jesus was given to us even before we were born, so that ultimately, if we believe in Christ, we will not perish, but be with God forever. This is love. This is God's love for you!

You may have thought you couldn't go on. Not one more day living the way you do. Maybe you have an illness that takes all your strength. You might experience pain daily, and wish your life would end. Or maybe you have monthly expenses and no money to pay for them. Maybe you have regrets and shame like I did, and feel like you can't go on. God has grace for anything that we are suffering right now.

II Corinthians 12:9 (Amplified Bible)

"But He said to me, My grace (My favor and loving-kindness and mercy) is enough for you [sufficient against any danger and enables you to bear the trouble manfully]; for My strength and power are made perfect) fulfilled and completed) and show themselves most effective in [your] weakness. Therefore, I will all the more gladly glory in my weaknesses and infirmities, that the strength and power of Christ (the Messiah) may rest (yes, may pitch a tent over and dwell upon me!)"

God's grace is there for us. Take it. Apply it to your situation, and live in it. It's when we are weak; we realize we need someone or something stronger than we are. God is bigger than anything you are going through. Admit you are weak to God. I know He will strengthen you. You see, nothing is impossible with God. No circumstance is too dark, or too out of control that God can't fix, if we let Him. He is there ready to give us His strength; we just need to ask for it.

Philippians 4:13 (Amplified Bible)

"I have strength for all things in Christ who empowers me [I am ready for anything through Him who infuses inner strength into me; I am self-sufficient in Christ's sufficiency]."

Maybe you don't know what to do. You are in the middle of a mess, and don't know which way to go to get out of it. Maybe you have to make a decision about an important, life-changing matter. You've tried to figure it out on your own, and can't.

Proverbs 3:5-7 (Amplified bible)

"Lean on, trust in, and be confident in the Lord with all your heart and mind and do not rely on your own insight or understanding. In all your ways know, recognize, and acknowledge Him, and He will direct and make straight and plain your paths. Be not wise in your own eyes; reverently fear and worship the Lord and turn [entirely] away from evil."

Acknowledging God is taking your circumstance before the Lord in prayer and asking Him what you should do. You are acknowledging the fact that you need to know God's opinion on the matter, and want to follow his direction. God will show you what you should do if you just ask Him. His answers will come in ways that you'll understand and recognize. Just relax and rest in His peace (Philippians 4:6 & 7 NKJV).

Negative thoughts continuously plagued me until I looked to God's word. Why is it that we allow our minds to race over the negative and not the positive? One thought that raced over and over in my mind was, "I will always have this mark of sin on me." Everywhere I go, people will see on my forehead what I did, and I will never be rid of it.

I John 1:9 (Amplified Bible)

"If we [freely] admit that we have sinned and confess our sins, He is faithful and just (true to His own nature and promises) and will forgive our sins [dismiss our lawlessness] and [continuously] cleanse us from all unrighteousness [everything not in conformity to His will in purpose, thought, and action]."

We are continuously cleansed from all unrighteousness! This makes me think of a clear glass of mud that is placed under a water faucet with the water continuously pouring into it. The mud starts to turn to muddy water, and as the water is still pouring into the glass, the water turns crystal clean. The mud is totally gone and this cleansing water continues to pour on us day in and day out, for the rest of our lives.

One of our biggest battlegrounds is our thought life. Take charge of it. It won't take care of itself. Don't dwell on the negative thoughts that come into your mind. Tell the Devil he's a liar! Speak truth to your heart with God's word. It will help you stand and to go on from day to day. Change your own self-image. The way you used to think about yourself is dead and gone.

Often times we don't feel good about ourselves and it's hard to break that way of thinking. Take the scriptures in this chapter and plaster them all over your house. I printed them from my computer and placed them all over where I would see them. I had to have something to remind me of who I really was, instead of what the lies were telling me! "Don't wait until you feel positive about yourself to move forward. Act your way into feeling good. That's the only way to start thinking more positively about your self."[7]

Every time I felt negative about myself, I took what the word of

God said about me, and I spoke out the truths of which I really was. When I thought I was never going to change, I said to myself, "I am a new creation! The old is past and the new has come," (II Corinthians 5:17 Amplified Bible [paraphrased]). When I felt people only saw the sinful mark on my forehead, I repeated "I am continuously cleansed from all the wrong I have done," I John 1:9 (Amplified bible [paraphrased]). When I was reminded of the guilt and shame, I would say, "...forgetting those things which are behind and reaching forward to those things which are ahead," (Philippians 3:13b NKJV). In time, I started to believe it.

I believe this will help those who are depressed and suicidal. I know from experience where my thoughts were right before trying to kill myself. All I listened to were the thoughts in my head, which were lies of no hope. If you are depressed or even feel like you want to end your life, try meditating on God's word and the promises He has for you.

Don't dwell on the negative. If you are depressed right now, you are extremely negative in your thought life. I'm sure you feel like there's no hope for your situation, but there is. The Devil wants you to believe you are different from other people. He wants you to isolate yourself from others. Do you feel like you always want to be alone? If so, this is not healthy. The Devil wants you to dwell on how you feel rather then what God's word says is true. You have to take hold of those thoughts and see them for what they are. No matter how long you've been depressed, make yourself read God's word and study what it promises you personally! Dig deep into scripture about joy, and rejoicing. Look at verses about hope and peace. You have to make yourself do this, even if you don't want to or think it will help. The truth is, it will help. This is a battle you have to win to survive. You won't get out of your depression by doing what you've always done. You have to do something different. I'm living proof it works. You are worth saving. The word of God grew in my spirit and it became a part of me and who I am today. Give it a try. It will change your life!

Chapter 4

STEP 2: FACING THE CONSEQUENCES

So Many Regrets

Of all the chapters I've written, this is one of the hardest. Looking back at what I had worked for and what God had given me, and then having it all taken from me is extremely painful.

Being a woman in ministry has been a struggle. Although God has opened doors that only I could walk through, I've also often felt that if I were male, I would have had more opportunities to teach God's word. The church has come a long way from the old tradition of only male ministers. But it still has a long way to go for women to feel total freedom to minister and walk in their gifts and the calling God has given them.

It took a long time for me to become an Associate Pastor. I never thought I'd ever be a pastor. It's amazing how God works, if we let Him, as He changes our desires and goals to match what He wants for our lives.

I started ministry as a singer, leading worship in my youth group at the age of fifteen. I also sang solo songs at my church from time to time. I started writing music around the age of nine, but never did anything with it until after I married Ron. He encouraged me to sing and to write my songs. He also encouraged me to work for my minister's license, so I did. In 1997, I became licensed with a major denomination and became a Minister of Music at various churches.

Leading Praise and Worship has always been close to my heart. Seeing people worshiping the Lord and lost in His love fueled me. I was given the opportunity to start a choir at a church and found that choir directing was easy and a joy to do. I even formed a Christian band called "Vertical Response," and we toured and ministered all across the Pacific Northwest. But I had always had a passion to preach and share the word of God. I enjoy delivering God's word to people, to encourage them in their journey and to impart truths to them.

Ron and I traveled from 1993 to 1994, touring the Pacific Northwest at various churches, camps, retreats, and conferences. I even ministered on radio and television. I wrote and recorded two CD's entitled, "A Righteous Life," and "Seasons of Change." After touring, I went on staff at several churches in Washington State, as Minister of Music and Associate Pastor.

Leading up to the church I was at when I made my mistake, I believe God was preparing me to become a pastor. I didn't know how it would come about, but I did know God was impressing in my heart often about shepherding his sheep. I was given the opportunity to become an Associate Pastor at a church of about 150-180 people. I learned a great deal. God was doing much in and through me! My schedule became crazy and I found myself at the church more than at home. This was when the enemy attacked me, hard. Looking back, I wish the people at the church had prayed for me more. We should always pray for our pastors. We don't know what the pastors are going through. I can't stress this enough. Pastors are on the front lines of battle every day. In addition to trying to minister to those in need, they are constantly being bombarded with deadlines, paper work and unfinished tasks that pile up. They want to give, but many times have given all they can and are still expected to give more. They are human just like you are. They go to sleep and wake up each day like you do. They have families that need them, just like you do. They make mistakes, just like you do. Hold them up in prayer. Your prayer might be exactly what prevents them from burning out or making a mistake like I did.

I offer this to show you what steps I took in ministry, and how much I lost because of falling into temptation. After my failure, I lost my job and had to resign. Everything that was connected to it was stripped from me. The only thing in ministry that was not taken from me was my band. The band members embraced and loved my husband and I through the process of healing and restoration.

BONDAGE OF SIN

The biggest consequence that immediately happens when one falls into temptation is the bondage of sin. Satan entices and tempts you with something that looks appealing to you at the time. There might be extenuating circumstances surrounding the reason why you gave in to temptation, but none-the-less you're in bondage. The moment you fall to the temptation, there is death of some sort. It might be death of a relationship or death of a thought process, or even physical death of someone. With my failure, I experienced death of who I was and what I stood for. My freedom, liberty and joy in Christ were immediately taken away. You see, "The wages of sin is death..." (Romans 6:23 NKJV). When I had read that scripture in the past, I always equated it to my past life without Christ, but Romans 6:23 applies to all people, whether or not they know Christ.

When a believer falls into temptation, there are so many "deaths" that take place. First and most importantly, sin separates us from God.

Isaiah 59:2 (NKJV)
"But your iniquities have separated you from your God; and your sins have hidden His face from you, so that He will not hear."

When we step forward with sin, we take a huge step away from God. God is still there; it is we sinners who've moved. Our actions have consequences. The biggest consequence of my action was separation from God. I tied God's hands from doing anything good in my life until I repented and turned from the wrong I was doing. I stopped God's blessings. I stopped God from hearing my cry, until I repented and confessed. We have to take responsibility for what we've done. We can't blame it on someone else and say, "If they didn't do this, I wouldn't have done that." God wants to see you take responsibility for your actions. Don't worry about what others have done. Just deal with what you've done, and God will deal with the rest. What is your part in the sin? If you've hurt someone, can you do anything to reconcile? It takes time to rebuild trust. Asking forgiveness is like buying a gift and wrapping it up in your best gift-wrap, and placing a beautiful bow on the top. You hope the other person will receive it, but there is a chance they won't. What they do with it is up to them, you've done your part in asking. That's all God wants from us, a willing humble heart.

How do you feel when you've sinned? What were your actions or reactions after you've sinned? Did you feel trapped? Being in bondage is not a fun place. You're full of shame, pain, guilt and regret. You're always trying to hide what you've done and you feel like everyone knows your mistake, which can separate you from people. When you confess to God, and possibly to those who need your confession, you immediately feel a release. The bondage and control the enemy had on you is lifted. Satan works in secret, and as long as you keep your sin in secret, he has control over you. As soon as you confess, the bondage is lifted and the control is broken.

WHAT DOES GOD DO WITH OUR SIN?

During this time in my life a popular song was being played on Christian radio. It talked about our sin being at the bottom of the sea. I would hear the song and ask God, "Is that really true? Is my sin gone because it is at the bottom of the ocean?" I did some research to see if the song was really Biblical. What I found out was astounding!

1. God Casts Our Iniquities into the Deep Sea!

Micah 7:19 (NKJV)
"He will again have compassion (loving kindness) on us. And will subdue our iniquities. You will cast all our sins into the depths of the sea."

It was true! My sin was at the bottom of the ocean, never to be seen or brought up again! After further praying and thinking more about that verse, God showed me something. If a person brings a drowning victim out of the water, who's been in for over twenty minutes, and attempts to bring him back to life, the victim will be brain dead, a vegetable for the rest of his life. He'll have no interaction with people, no thought process, no living, as he knew it before. That's no life at all.

This is what God showed me about my sin. He hurled, thrust, and literally cast it, with His powerful right arm, into the sea. If someone tried to bring it back up again to revive it, they would be trying to revive a corpse. There would be no life in it. Actually, they would look foolish for trying to do so and the shame they possibly wanted to bring on me, could fall on them. After we confess and repent, our sin is dead! It's at the bottom of the sea, never to be seen or brought up again. It's unfortunate that man remembers the sin, but God never does.

2. God Will Not Remember Our Sin Again.

Isaiah 43:25 (Amplified Bible)
"I, even I, am He who blots out and cancels your transgressions, for your sake, and I will not remember your sins."

How awesome is that! God proposes to never remember our sins, ever again! Thank God for His incredible grace that's always waiting for us.

What can we do with the shame and regret we experience after we have sinned?

3. He Covers Our Sin!

Psalm 32:1 (Amplified Bible)
"Blessed (Happy, fortunate, to be envied) is he who has forgiveness of his transgression continually exercised upon him, whose sin is covered."

Our sin is totally covered by God. His forgiveness is continually exercised upon us, always! We have to get hold of that. It is truth! We are forgiven and our sin is covered, period! No questions asked! If we read further on in Psalm 32 it gets even better.

Psalm 32:2-8 (Amplified Bible)
"Blessed (happy, fortunate, to be envied) is the man to whom the Lord imputes no iniquity and in whose spirit there is no deceit. When I

kept silence [before I confessed], my bones wasted away through my groaning all the day long for day and night Your hand [of displeasure] was heavy upon me; my moisture was turned into the drought of summer. Selah [pause, and calmly think of that]! I acknowledged my sin to You, and my iniquity I did not hide. I said, I will confess my transgressions to the Lord [continually unfolding the past till all is told]—then You [instantly] forgave me the guilt and iniquity of my sin. Selah [pause, and calmly think of that]! For this [forgiveness] let everyone who is godly pray—pray to you in a time when You may be found; surely when the great waters [of trial] overflow, they shall not reach [the spirit in] him. You are a hiding place for me; You. Lord, preserve me from trouble, You surround me with songs and shouts of deliverance. Selah [pause, and calmly think of that]! I [the Lord] will instruct you and teach you in the way you should go; I will counsel you with My eye upon you."

God will counsel us and He always has His eye on us. I am so thankful for a place to hide and be accepted and forgiven. The only place is in the arms of God. If you are experiencing unforgiveness or rejection from others, run to the forgiving, loving arms of God! He will never reject you and will always forgive you. There is always acceptance in His arms.

4. God Removes, or Takes Away Our Sin from Us!

Psalm 103:12 (NKJV)
"As far as the east is from the west, so far has He removed our transgressions from us."

John 1:29 (NKJV)
"The next day John saw Jesus coming toward him, and said, 'Behold! The Lamb of God who takes away the sin of the world.'"

Our sins are no longer there! God has removed them completely from us. He has taken them away from us altogether. We are the ones who need to let them go. When you think of your past or the enemy reminds you of your past, say, "Its gone, dead, cast, even hurled into the sea where there's no life left in it."

5. God Has Swept Away Our Offenses and Sin.

Isaiah 44:22 (NIV)
"I have swept away your offenses like a cloud, your sins like the morning mist."

Isaiah 44:22 in the Amplified Bible states, "He has blotted out like a thick cloud your transgressions, and like a cloud your sins." It's all in God's power, not ours. For there's nothing we can do that will make our sins go away and our broken, messed up past be gone; only God has the power to do so. This brings hope and joy! We can walk in victory knowing God has done this in our lives.

These scriptures are not for the good people who've never sinned. "For all have sinned and fall short of the glory of God." (Romans 3:23) These scriptures are for you and me, sinners saved by His grace!

It took a long time for me to really understand what God did with my sin. I had so many regrets, and those regrets were constantly in my face. I was reminded daily, even minute by minute, of what I'd done and what I'd lost. But these scriptures have helped me to grab hold of the truth about God and what He has done with my sin... forever!

There were so many regrets and consequences I experienced after my failure. Again, I thought God would wipe them all away. I was waiting for God to restore my circumstances and me immediately. God had another plan. I had to walk through the consequences of my sin so the sting of them would prevent me from ever going down the same path again. Also, we never realize how our sin affects others. Here are a few of the consequences I experienced.

THE LOSS OF MONEY

When I had to resign as associate pastor, the paychecks stopped coming in. I never had to resign from anything in my life. I usually was the one who made the decision to leave a place of employment. This time, it was out of my hands and I couldn't fix it. I couldn't look for a job because of my emotional state. I could hardly get through the day, let alone try to work somewhere. Our finances were hit hard. We also had hospital bills we had to pay for and ambulance expenses. The medical insurance I had was stopped after I had to resign, because it was through the church. We were left with so much debt. The impact of my mistake was felt in every area of our lives. This was a huge consequence for my sin that I never imagined.

THE LOSS OF FRIENDS

Most of our friends were at the church where I served. When we had to leave, all those friendships gradually stopped. It was hard and painful. Members of the church didn't know all the details of my failure. People can be very critical. It was easier to walk away from the friendships than to try to continue them. Most of them broke away from me. Even my closest friends stopped contact. It was hard on my family. My daughters were very young and didn't understand why they couldn't be with their friends at church anymore. The consequences of sin reach and stretch beyond what you can ever imagine. It not only affected me, but my family, my church family, and I am sure more than I even know today.

Satan makes the wrong look right and the right looks wrong to get us to fall into temptation. He never tells you how it will effect you or the ones you love. I pray my candidness will prevent someone from making the same mistake I did. Sin is never worth what the Devil tells you it's worth. No, he never tells you the cost of your sin. He only tells you what you could possibly enjoy, or you'd never sin. There has to be some pleasure in sin, or we'd never do it. Looking back, I can't even imagine what I was thinking, to do what I did. I'm so different now. God has changed me, as I yielded to Him and His correction. I'm a totally new creation. My old way of thinking is gone, and I have a renewed mind in Christ, who helps me make right decisions for each new day. It's all due to laying down my will and asking God to have His way, not mine. Now, it has been many years since my failure. I find myself saying under my breath, "Have Your way." and "Thank You, Lord!" or "You are a good God!" Not even realizing it, I'm constantly praising Him throughout the day. That is how much He has restored my mind. I don't think the same, act the same, or even want to do the same things I did before I failed.

Where are you? What are you thinking right now? Are your thoughts pleasing to God? Are you being tempted to do something you know is not right? Don't listen to the Devil's lies. If you feel conviction over what you are tempted to do right now, think before you do. The conviction is the Holy Spirit trying to help you make a good choice. If you follow through with the temptation, you will lose so much, including people you love and cherish. It's not worth it! Walk away from the temptation. It is better to pay the price now then to pay it later like I did.

THE LOSS OF MY INTEGRITY

This is a big one. My town wasn't extremely small, but it wasn't a big city like New York or Seattle. Word got around fast. All I had worked for, being a woman in ministry, was gone. All I had proved myself to be was gone. It was important to me that I was a woman of my word, my word was gone. That was another thing that pushed me over the edge to try to commit suicide. I was an approval addict. Now, people didn't approve of me. When people thought of my name, they thought of my sin. I knew it would take a long time for me to prove myself again--to my spouse, my family, and to those who knew me in ministry. Why should anyone trust me again? Why did God allow me to have a second chance? He did, and I'm thankful! I noticed God is willing to give second chances, when people are not. We need to keep our eyes on Jesus, not people, or our past. Whatever we are looking at, that's what we will pursue. I choose Christ!

THE LOSS OF MY MINISTER'S LICENSE

With the denomination I was licensed in, if they approved, they would place a fallen minister in rehabilitation. I was placed there. It was a two-year process. I was a year into the process when my case was re-opened. Ron and I were beginning to heal. We had a new beginning, and now the wound was opened again. It brought back all the shame and guilt I felt. It also effected Ron more than before.

I felt I could do something about the pain I caused my spouse this time. Ultimately feeling I had to make a choice between my husband and my minister's license, I chose my husband. I walked away from the possibility of being reinstated as a licensed minister. Unfortunately, my denomination looked at it as a dismissal and stated it as such. There was nothing I could do about the statement. Just knowing it was my decision to walk away instead of the district's, meant the world to me. I wish my old denomination was more personal and caring. It was surprising how they handled my leaving. I never received a phone call from the district that I was held accountable to the year before. They never contacted me with concern or care. I just received a letter stating I was dismissed. This was another thing I had to lay at Jesus' feet and leave there. Later, I became a licensed minister with another organization. They welcomed me with open arms, even knowing my failure. Thank God for second chances!

REBUILDING ME

This entire book is really an account of me being rebuilt from the inside out. From the refining fire seasons and discipline, to the resting and the making me lie down in green pastures, to the relearning of walking with baby steps which grew into bigger steps, it was all the process of healing I needed to go through. Thank God for His ever-present hand upon our lives for correction, restoration, and healing.

I believe we all want to think we're good and our views on life are always correct. Reality check: We're always under construction by God to mold and make us to be more like His Son. If we think more highly of ourselves, God will bring us through humility to show us our pride, arrogance, and our need for Him.

Proverbs 16:18 (KJV)
"Pride goeth before destruction, and a haughty spirit before a fall."

Romans 12:3 (KJV)
"For I say, through the grace given unto me, to every man that is among you, not to think of himself more highly than he ought to think; but to think soberly, according as God hath dealt to everyman the measure of faith."

So, I welcome the correcting hand of God and His constant carving knife on my life. I do want to be more like Him daily. The process of rebuilding me, I believe, is still ongoing today. But, there was an intensive refining fire stage at the very beginning of walking out of failure that was extremely hot and painful. God brought me to a place of showing me areas in my life that needed to change. I remember telling people, "You know how God brings you along in life and suddenly He shows you one area that needs changing, like your attitude? Then you yield to Him and He starts changing you and you go on for a few more years and another area of your life is shown that needs correction? God is constantly showing me one thing after another. When will He stop and let me breath?"

I'm glad God didn't stop. My pump was primed and ready for His correction and God felt it necessary to correct me a great deal then. God pricked my heart to look at one thing after another. I would spend hours on my face before God, crying out to Him and asking Him to change me. I know He was pruning me and purging me. I call those times, "God Wrestlings." This is when God is speaking to our hearts to give up an area or change something in us, and we struggle. The anointing of the Holy Spirit will be there immediately to help bring about the change that needs to take place. This takes time. As you allow God those areas of your heart, change will slowly come because God is faithful to finish His work He started in you.

I came to a place in my prayer life where I just said, "Burn it all out, God! Burn out the dross in me until it is all gone. I want to be pure before You and pleasing in Your sight."

We might have sung songs in church that ask God to change or purify our heart, or make us more like Jesus. Do we really know what we are asking and singing? God will take us up on our words. Are we willing to pay the cost to be more like Him? The flesh has to die which says, "I want my will and my way." We must decrease so he can increase! We've heard that statement many times before, but it is true. We have to decrease. Our will has to step aside so God can have control and increase in us. I look back and am thankful for the refining fire season. I know I will have more of those seasons; it's just part of getting closer to Him. But now, I embrace them because I know that only good comes out of those times as I draw close and let God's fire refine me to be more like His Son!

SABOTAGING MYSELF

Probably the most difficult thing to overcome in our walk out of failure is our negative self-image, and the mental battle that constantly occurs in our minds. We can sabotage our future by how we deal with situations that come up from day to day. We might see someone from our past and automatically think, "They know everything about my failure, I know they think poorly of me and they've talked about me to other people." This has come up often in my journey of walking out of failure. It took me a long time, mostly by my husband, Ron, reminding me, "You don't know what the other person is thinking or how they have responded." I would always come to the worst conclusion that this person knows everything and thinks poorly of me.

First of all, it doesn't matter what people think. It only matters what Jesus Christ thinks. I'm not saying there are no consequences of our sins, for there always are. After I had asked for forgiveness and dealt with the consequences, I would come across people who were connected somehow to my past and would respond to them from what I thought they were thinking. In other words, in my mind, I had already come to the conclusion they thought poorly of me and I would put up a wall or ignore them. This sabotaged a lot of friendships and relationships. I remember ministering on a worship team for a woman's retreat, and I saw several people from the church I resigned from at the retreat. Some had been in the lady's Bible study class I taught when I was their pastor. In my mind, I had already come to the conclusion they didn't like me, that they felt I shouldn't be ministering ever again. I avoided them and tried not to talk to them because of what they might say to me. They ended up coming up to me and expressed how much they missed me and wished I was back ministering at their church, saying that, "The church wasn't the same without me there." This was only one of many situations that happened.

I am determined not to sabotage my future with how I look at myself or how I think people look at me. One of the reasons I tried to commit suicide is that I thought people were not pleased with me. Realizing this made me determined not to end up on the road of self-destruction again. I was determined to conquer the battle in my mind when it came up. My past is what I was, but not who I am today. As I hold onto Christ and the cross of Calvary, and stay obedient to His word the best I can, I believe God is directing me and guiding me to a beautiful future. The best is yet to come!

What if those people I ran across did know exactly what I did and gossiped about it to other people? As long as I went to God with my feelings, I was all right. The moment I picked it up and stewed about it, I was a mess, emotionally. God showed me that they'd be held accountable for their actions too. If they judged me, it was sin. Sin is sin and they will be held accountable. They will have consequences to walk through because of their sin. I pray for mercy on them as God has shown mercy to me.

There is a story about a sinful woman who came and poured her costly perfumed oil onto Jesus' feet (Luke 7:36-50 NKJV). I wrote an Easter drama two years after my failure and this story was acted out. The drama was called, "His Incredible Grace." One of the scenes depicts the immoral woman who came and poured out her precious perfumed oil over Christ's feet and kissed and washed them with her tears. The Pharisees, especially Simon, judged her harshly for doing such an act. How could Jesus allow this woman to touch Him when she was a sinner? How often have we quickly judged someone when we don't know what they've gone through, or what cost they've paid? The cost for the sinful woman's oil was a past history of immorality; no doubt, that's how she paid for the perfumed oil in the first place. The cost was the shame and judgment she felt from herself and people. She lived for years with no hope of ever changing her lifestyle. Now, she came to pour it all out on Jesus. She poured it on the One who forgave her of all the wrong she had done. This is love in action on her part.

I know what this woman felt as the Pharisees looked at her with judgmental eyes. I know the pain she experienced hearing the whispers of criticism. Yet, Jesus forgave her and washed away all her past right before those who judged her. This is what Jesus did for me as I poured out all my tears of regret and shame to Him. He covers our mistakes. He always loves and accepts us. We cannot change our past, but we can change our future. We can do this by following Jesus, walking in His ways, and by being totally honest with Him, pliable, and open to change.

CONCLUSION OF ALL MY REGRETS AND CONSEQUENCES

Looking back, I could have lost so much more than what I've described here. I could've lost my husband and access to my children. I could've lost my life through suicide, and not have written this book. Thank God for His powerful intervention in my life! Thank God for changing the course to where I was headed. That's His mercy and grace!

Regrets are heavy. They're like weighted balls of steel connected to chains that are wrapped around our necks. "If only" and "should have" will strangle us if we let it. We are the only ones who can let go of those chains. We have the power to let go. It's a day to day process, but it can be done with God's help. Christ died for all our regrets and shame. We can walk in liberty by letting go of our past and reaching forward to a wonderful future in Christ. A new beginning is waiting for you, take it!

Chapter 5

STEP 3: GIVING UP CONTROL

More of You and Less of Me

Our flesh wants to be in control. We want what we want, and we want it now! After all, allowing God to have control, with His time and purposes, takes too long. We "help God out" by going ahead with our ideas and agendas to make change happen. Even if God gave us the vision, often we try to hurry up the process. But, all we end up doing is making a mess of our lives.

We find this human character trait in Sarah, Abraham's wife. God had promised Abraham he would be the father of a great nation. Abraham's descendants would be as the sand on the seashore. How could this be? He and Sarah had never had any children. Now he was old and she was well past her childbearing years. Genesis 16 shows us what happens when we try to make something happen in our time instead of waiting on God for His time and purpose. Sarah had her Egyptian maid, Hagar, conceive Abraham's child and Ishmael was born. Eventually, in God's time, He allowed Sarah to conceive and Isaac was born. The two brothers fought, and their descendants fight to this very day. I could go on in much more detail, but I think you get the idea. When we don't wait for God's time, and try to make things happen in our own time, only mistakes are made. Waiting is one of the hardest things for us humans to do, but when we do, we are blessed.

Our self-sufficiency will destroy us and our pride will prevent

God's favor and blessing in our lives. The flesh is hard to tame. The only thing that will tame it is to lay it down at Christ's feet and say, "Have your way in me." Christ said it well in Matthew 26:39b Amplified Bible, "...My Father, if it is possible, let this cup pass away from Me; nevertheless, not what I will [not what I desire], but as You will and desire." Even Jesus gave up control to the Father when He literally laid down His life for His Father's will.

The process of surrendering our all to Christ is a difficult and painful process, yet extremely rewarding once we do it. For me, the process took time. I fought God on this issue. It was not until I was firmly confronted by someone that I realized I was fighting to keep control of my life. It surfaced one day and my reaction was ugly. How could I give up control? Maybe a better question would be, "When did I take back control of my life after I asked Christ into my heart as my Lord and Savior?" If I gave God back control, I might lose my position in ministry. I might become someone I didn't want to become, or do something I didn't want to do.

I spent a good portion of my life building up what I wanted to have happen instead of waiting on God for His time and what He wanted for me. I realized my self-worth was wrapped up in what I did, not in who I was in Christ. I had to face myself, or as the Bible calls it, my "flesh," and what I saw was not a pretty sight. My right to myself had to be broken. "For to me, to live is Christ, and to die is gain," Philippians 1:21 (NKJV). Galatians 2:20 (NKJV) states, "I have been crucified with Christ; it is no longer I who live, but Christ lives in me; and the life which I now live in the flesh I live by faith in the Son of God, who loved me and gave Himself for me." These passages of scripture show how we are to view our lives. It's all about what He wants. We are not our own, when we give our hearts to Christ, we are His.

I had to lay my dreams and goals at Christ's feet. They were my crowns, or the precious things I had carried all my life, and really they amounted to nothing compared to God's plans for me. I have to say that I was frustrated and angry at this point in my life. I really fought God and struggled for some time on giving God back control, but ultimately, all my frustration was getting me nowhere. It was just a dead end road that I kept traveling on. I gave God back control of my life and said, 'Have your way in me, even if it hurts," and it did hurt.

You need to deal with your flesh immediately. Your flesh doesn't want to die. It will scream out at you to stop. It will scream out in self-pity to have its way. Be aware of it when the time comes for you to let go of your control to God. If self-pity wins, sin has won. Press through the pain of letting go of your will.

The world will tell you to look out for yourself, stand up for your rights, but God requires us to be broken and have a contrite heart, these sacrifices God will never despise (Psalm 51:17 NKJV). It's never fun to die. It costs us something. Our will has to die. Flesh wants to run when it is costly or painful.

I like how the Amplified Bible states Galatians 2:20: "I am crucified with Christ [in Him I have shared His crucifixion]; it is no longer I who live, but Christ (the Messiah) lives in me; and the life I now live in the body I live by faith in (by adherence to and reliance on and complete trust in) the Son of God, Who loved me and gave Himself up for me."

We must die to our flesh, our pride, and self-sufficiency, because they can rob us of a close relationship with Christ, and prevent us from being what God created us to be. Amy Wilson, with the Christian Literature Crusade, expresses this thought well;

> God, harden me against myself,
> The coward with pathetic voice
> Who craves for ease and rest and joy.
> Myself, arch-traitor to myself,
> My hollowest friend,
> My deadliest foe,
> My clog, whatever road I go.[8]

Our flesh will scream to have its way. We are only deceiving our self if we let it win. Part of our flesh is our pride. Pride comes in so many packages. One big package was my stubborn will.

WHAT IS BROKENNESS?

I think brokenness is more an attitude than an incident. There are many elements to brokenness. First it is a state of true humility. We can try and be humble, but true humility is realizing our need for God. It is a knowing that life evolves around Him and not us. True humility is a heart that wants to continually please God first and foremost above our own needs and wants. One interesting thing about true humility is it proves itself. It proves the one whom it represents. In other words, if we are walking in true humility, we will not want to be always seen, or to be first in line, or to be expecting others to wait on us. True humility will look out for the interests of others instead of always looking out for itself. Jesus said it well when he spoke to the Scribes and Pharisees saying, "But he who is greatest among you shall be your servant. And whoever exalts himself will be humbled, and he who humbles himself will be exalted" (Matthew 23:10-11 NJKV). A true sign of humility is a person who is willing to serve, even when no one is looking. Are you a true humble servant?

Another attribute of brokenness is the absence of pride. There is a certain kind of pride that has a "look at me" spirit attached to it. When you see it in others, it leaves a sick feeling in the pit of your stomach. I've encountered it many times as a worship leader working with a worship team. Satan fell from heaven because of his pride (Isaiah 14:12-15). I can see why worship teams struggle and even churches struggle over what kind of music is to be played at church. This battle has been going on for generations and generations.

When working with worship teams, I have found that the members who have pride built up in their hearts are the hardest to work with. The truly broken, humble members will want to help out in any way to bring in the presence of God. Prideful members will want to be seen and want to have their way. One thing I've noticed with those members that have pride in their hearts is eventually they will have to choose between two choices. Either they will finally notice the pride in their hearts and want to change, or they will harden their hearts and continue deeper in their pride. This could possibly lead to destruction in their lives.

Proverbs 16:18 (NKJV)
"Pride goes before destruction, and a haughty spirit before a fall."

I remember praying one morning, shortly after my failure, and in my mind's eye I could see a big pile of gray rags. From the pile of rags was rising a stream of steam. This showed stench. This was my righteousness. I knew it immediately. The closer I got to the pile, the uglier it became to me. God started to reveal what my righteousness was. Times when I took the glory for His talents I possessed. Times when my prayers were answered for those that I prayed for, and I felt it was my doing. Times of preaching and people praising me for how it ministered to them. One thing after another God began to show me. One by one I asked Him to forgive me. I finally said to God, "We need to do some laundry!" He lovingly spoke, "No! Throw it all away." I needed to throw it all in the garbage. God had his righteousness available for me to wear, mine was as filthy rags (Isaiah 64:6 KJV).

Since receiving first hand the destruction from my own pride, I've tried to warn other people of this possibility, but the only true school is the school of hard knocks. We all have to live it to really understand it. Pride is an element that will defile us if never addressed. It's easy to allow pride to build and grow in our hearts. I did it and shrugged it off, as it was not important to look at. I didn't think I had a lot of pride in me. Wow, was I deceived. It was eating away at me and I never saw it.

Mark 7:20-23 (NKJV)

"And He (Jesus) said, 'What comes out of a man, that defiles a man. For from within, out of the heart of men, proceed evil thoughts, adulteries, fornications, murders, thefts, covetousness, wickedness, deceit, lewdness, an evil eye, blasphemy, pride, foolishness. All these evil things come from within and defile a man."

We should never think we could handle pride. Always lay the compliment people give you at the foot of the cross and leave it there. These "jewels" that were given to you are really Christ's.

There is much grace for those that rid pride from their lives. It is an on going process. We will always be tempted with pride, especially if you are in ministry of some sort. Practice laying it down before Christ. This will help you to guard it from your heart.

After pride was revealed in my heart, brokenness came. I saw and smelled the stench of my righteousness. I have seen first hand what my pride caused in the lives of so many people. Brokenness comes when we arrive at the end of ourselves. I arrived there from my own hands of my suicide attempt. How could I have come to that place? I use to be able to trust myself in hard times. Never did I think I would ever try and kill myself. The thought of it brings shivers down my spine even now. It has been many years now since that dreadful dark time in my life. But, from that time, came brokenness in my heart that needed to come. I've thought long and hard about brokenness and what it really means.

BROKENNESS IS...

... The realization of who I am compared to God.
... A true humility and submissive heart to God.
... A heart's cry of desperation to a loving God.
... Waiting on God's time, not mine.
... Laying down my crowns and dreams for God's.
... Not wanting my will, but God's.
... Letting go of my control to God.
... A heart of obedience and thankfulness towards God.
... A realization of my self-righteousness compared to God's.
... A knowing that I'm lost without God.

I'd love to say I came to the place of brokenness through my own wisdom and know-how, but it took this failure in my life to bring me to the end of me. When I arrived there, I had no other place to turn, but to God. I finally saw my desperate need for Him. The desire to be obedient to His will flooded my heart. After I gave back control to God, I found my burden was lifted, my anger was gone, and life seemed easier and lighter. Often it does take us getting to the end of ourselves to give up and seek God's help. His ways are far better than our ways. God knows what is best for us.

Our self-sufficiency gets us in trouble every time. Look at Peter. He was full of self-sufficiency. It was not until Peter failed and denied Christ three times, that he saw his weakness.

As pastors we can easily fall into the trap of routine. We do the same thing week after week, and probably could do it with a blindfold on and our hands tied behind our backs. What my experience tells me is that this is a trap the enemy wants all ministers to fall into. Often it is through our failures that we see such things in our lives. God has a way of taking our failure, if we let Him, and make something beautiful of it. He has done it in me and He can and will do it in you. Will you let him? I believe it is a day to day dying to ourselves, and constantly laying our crowns at the feet of the One who bore the most painful crown for us all!

Why is it important to be broken before the Lord? The importance is in the fact that God can use broken things more than He can use rigid things. There are many examples of brokenness and how God used it. Jesus was broken, yielding to His heavenly Father's wishes instead of His own. (Luke 22:42) He allowed His precious body to be broken for all of us. He took the five loaves of bread and broke them to feed the huge crowd (Mark 8:1-10). The sinful woman brought the costly perfumed oil and broke it and poured it on Christ's feet. It meant nothing until she broke it open and poured it out for her Savior (Matthew 26:7, Mark 14:3, Luke 7:37).

God uses broken things. Brokenness causes repentance and desperation for Him. There has to be a deep brokenness in us to experience all that God has for us. Broken vessels for His glory. Relying upon His sufficiency not ours. This moves the heart of God.

At the point of my brokenness, all I could do was cry. When people would come and talk to me about my failure, I was tearfully broken. I couldn't stop the tears. One day I was having a conversation with a pastor's wife on the phone, and all I could do was cry. I finally told her, "All I have to offer is brokenness." I ended our conversation and wept. "Why do I cry all the time, Lord?" I asked.

His response was very gentle and loving. I felt an overwhelming sense that I was exactly where God wanted me to be. I was broken and it was a good thing. I used to hate crying in front of people, now I welcomed the tears. Knowing God could use broken things brought hope in my heart that God would use me again. I offered my tears as a sacrifice that day to God. He received it with open arms and comforted me in the middle of my emotional pain. I felt my offering was nothing compared to what others offered God. Yet it was all I could offer at that time. It was my "widow's mite." (Mark 12:42-44) So I offered it, all of my mistakes, all of the hurt I caused, all the pain of my regrets, and all of my past. I asked God to multiply it for His glory. I knew God could multiply, what seemed to be nothing, into something. I was down to nothing, but God was up to something! As I offered it all that day, I wrote the song; "Brokenness." [see page 52]

MORE OF YOU, LESS OF ME

I think the most significant realization in this entire journey was giving up control of my life again to God. This was so critical for change to come in me. God wants to bring about change in our lives, but we can tie God's hands. Until we let go and let God have His way, God can do very little with our lives. You see, right after my failure, and after I came back from the hospital, I still was in control. The battle continued in me for days. It was about a month and a half after I had come home from the hospital that I came face to face with this issue. A friend brought it up, and as I said before, I fought it and struggled with it. I was mad at my friend for bringing it up. God was bringing me through the refining fire and this was part of the heat and fire I had to endure.

This issue had to be addressed. I knew my friend was right. I remember being in a church parking lot as my friend shared what I needed to do to go on from where I was. I asked her, "How can I give up control?"

She promptly went to her hands and knees, on an extremely hot summer day, on blistering asphalt in the church parking lot, and cried, "Have Your way. I give up control of my life. If You want me to do nothing for the rest of my life, I will do nothing. If You want me to scrub toilets, I will scrub toilets. I surrender everything to You."

The thought of it, even now, brings tears to my eyes. When did I take back control? Not only did I take back control, but I also had a very strong grip on the steering wheel and was not about to let go. I left my friend, as she was kneeling in the church parking lot, and walked into the church. I laid down on one of the pews and wept and sobbed. I left the church and went home, angry with God for requiring this of me. Having control seemed the only thing I had left after being stripped of so many things. At least I was in control of my control. I know that might sound

BROKENNESS

By Kris Belfils

All I offer You Is my brokenness, brokenness and me
All that I can give Is my very life, the life You give to me
I would offer You my riches
I would offer You my righteousness
I would offer You my strength
But that is not what You desire

Oh take my offering, I will obey
All I offer You please multiply and use
I am broken, Lord; I offer You brokenness

All I offer You is my very need; My very need for You
All that I can give is my heart to change,
a heart for more of You
I would offer You my song
I would offer You my sacrifice
I would offer You my dreams
But that is not what You require

Why is what You desire... hard to give
Why is what You require... so high to pay

Still that is all I can offer You... I am Yours.

weird, but that was how I felt. Have you ever thought those words? I had no control over losing my position as an Associate Pastor. I had no control over losing my monthly salary. I had no control over what people thought of me. I had no control over my schedule and the isolation from people I was experiencing. Life consisted of staying home, crying most of the day, smothered in my regrets, and ashamed of bad choices and myself.

So here I was, stripped of everything I knew as my identity, unable to fix what I had done, and now God was asking me to give up my control. Later that night, I lay in my bed wanting to turn my back on God. I got up and went outside to my back yard. It was after midnight. I lifted my fist toward the sky and yelled at God for requiring this of me, cursing the day I was born. Looking back, I have to chuckle. Here was a grown woman in her pajamas, yelling at the top of her lungs, and shaking my fist up to the heavens. Yet, that was the breaking point in me. This was that dead end road I kept coming to. The road starts with a choice, leads to anger, and you are left with a decision to make. The last time I was on this road, I took a whole container of sleeping pills. This time my will started to break. I went to my knees and sobbed. I was holding on to my will and saw it was getting me nowhere. I could see how my past choices had led to self-destruction. It was a frightening place to be again. I fell to the ground and wept. I didn't want to end my life, but how could I give God control? I knew God was loving and patient. I knew God was for me and not against me. I knew I couldn't rely on my own understanding. I was determined to give God back control, but I wanted to do it in the morning, I was tired and exhausted. I went back in the house and back to my bed. Lying there, I said a quick prayer to God that I would talk to Him in the morning about it.

When I woke up the next day I knew in my heart that I was ready to give God control. I waited for my morning prayer time. It was like a dam had broken inside of me and I cried and cried to God. The realization that I needed God was huge. There was so much of me and hardly any of Him in me at that point. I gave up control-- all of it. The words "Have Your way in me!" permeated my very core. "HAVE YOUR WAY! HAVE YOUR WAY! Please, forgive me! GOD I NEED YOU IN MY LIFE! I CAN'T LIVE WITHOUT YOU! I SELF-DESTRUCT WITHOUT YOU, LORD!"

What a release I felt in my heart. I was free! God started to increase in me and I was finally decreasing! Up to that point, there was so much of me in the way. God couldn't do anything to change me because I wouldn't let Him. Now, God was free to help bring the healing. He had the open door to help renew my mind. He had the liberty to show me more and more areas of my heart that needed a transformation. My heart was now pliable soil to plant seeds of new life. The bondage I felt from the struggle was over. I wrote a song that day called, "I Am Free."

After I wrote it, I sang it over and over to Him, crying and laughing at the same time. I was free. God was in charge and it felt good. He was sweeter than He had ever been before. My love for Him came flooding into my heart and my desire to live for Him overwhelmed me. The burden of figuring out my life was gone. God was now in control and I would slowly start to learn how to trust His leading again. Even when I didn't see what I wanted to see, I could trust God's heart that He had a plan for my life and He would fulfill that plan. He knew I would fail, yet He had a plan. He knew the human race would sin, yet He had a plan. This plan was called Jesus Christ. I cannot express how freeing it was to give up control. I encourage you to do it in your life. Really look deep inside of who you are. Do you want your way, or do you truly trust God to direct your every step? I will talk more about trusting God in Chapter ten, "Help From the Psalms."

I AM FREE

By Kris Belfils

Take my life; take my heart
I am yours, all of me
Pour Yourself; pour Your love
More of You less of me

Hold my hand; hold me close
Under Your wings, all of me
There is peace; there is strength
I'm letting go; less of me

I am free, I am free
Soaring in Your love, I am free
I am free, I am free
Hold me in Your arms, I am free

Now I know, Now I see
Letting go frees me

Chapter 6

STEP 4: FORGIVING PEOPLE AND MYSELF

Dealing with Anger

As you read in Chapter 5, anger was the force behind my attempt to commit suicide. I was so angry with myself. Angry at the situation I was in. Angry that my life had come to where it was. The day I had to resign as Associate Pastor was the day I felt I could not go on. My focus was on me and my priorities were all out of order. It was a dark day; God seemed far away. I hadn't given myself back to Him. I was still in control. The struggle was still inside me.

I was angry with people, and particularly at a close friend for not supporting me when I needed her support the most. I felt betrayed by her and betrayed by myself for getting into the mess. Nothing I could do would change the situation. I was able to get myself out of jams before, but this time it seemed hopeless. All my attempts to fix the situation were futile and actually made things worse. I felt so hopeless and helpless. Instead of turning to Jesus, I was angry with Him as well. I know that sounds harsh, but I was. Satan had filled my mind with so many lies and I was listening to every word he said and believing them. That was the day I left home, bought sleeping pills, took all of them, parked my van in a grocery store parking lot, and called my husband and said "goodbye." Thank God He intervened and rescued me from my actions.

FORGIVENESS

Forgiving others when they've wronged you in some way is a hard thing to do. But forgiving others when you know you've done wrong, is a whole different story. When we've done wrong, we can't go back and undo what we did to try to fix a relationship or make the hurt go away. In my situation, there were a few people I confided in and asked for help to get out of the bondage connected with my failure. I trusted them to keep a confidence, but a part of my sin was revealed. To this day, I have to lay them at the cross and leave them there. In the end, I believe it was God's way of stopping me from continuing to walk down the wrong path I was on. Maybe you've trusted someone and they've let you down. We have to let go of the hurt we've experienced, and move on in Christ. If we don't, we will never get past any unforgiveness, and it will turn into hatred and bitterness.

I wish I had the answer to why people act the way they do. I can turn that thought back to me and ask, "Why did I make a bad choice and fall into temptation? Why wasn't I strong enough to overcome the temptation? Why didn't I run from what was tempting me? Why didn't I walk in integrity in front of my congregation instead of letting them down?" I do know that when we take a situation and look at it from our point of view instead of God's, we are relying on our own understanding. We only see what is right in front of us, but God sees the whole picture.

Proverbs 3:5 and 6 (Amplified Bible)

"Lean on, trust in, and be confident in the Lord with all your heart and mind and do not rely on your own insight or understanding. In all your ways know, recognize and acknowledge Him, and He will direct and make straight and plain your paths."

With this scripture in mind, I have to lean on God and trust Him with everything, including my relationships. For me, this was and still is hard, especially when it comes to those who have hurt me. Yet, when I place my hurts in God's hands, the burden I carry is lifted. It might not make my relationship better, but it does free me to let go. I know that's easier said than done. If we can just release our tight grip on our past,

God could start the healing process in us, and in all those involved.

I don't know how many times I've said, "I can't change what I've done. If I could, I would've a long time ago." I've cried out to God, "Lord, please heal the hurts I've caused others because of my failure." Only God can heal. I have to trust that He is healing those I've wronged, because the proof is in the fact that He is healing me. He loves those I've wronged and those who've wronged me. But, there's still an anger that creeps up in my heart from time to time which surprises me. This anger stems from my regrets and the process of forgiving myself.

"How could I have fallen?" "What was I thinking?" These thoughts have plagued me over and over again. At first, they consumed my mind. They rattled the very core of who I was. I thought I'd forgiven myself, but I would find myself not liking me. I would do something and then turn around and wish I'd never done it. My mind was unstable and so were my actions.

The process of wanting to live after attempting suicide was a long one. Every day I had to place my life in God's hands. Every day I had to ask God to help me find good in it, to get through that day. He did, and more. Some days were brighter than others. Just when I thought I was doing better emotionally, I would plummet to a dark place emotionally, and not want to go on living. I realized the core of it was that I'd not forgiven myself. The Bible says if we don't forgive, God won't forgive us. When I applied that verse to myself, my realization was huge.

Here are a few verses regarding forgiveness. Read the verses and think of any lack of forgiveness you might have towards yourself and others.

Mark 11:25 and 26 (Amplified Bible)

"And whenever you stand praying, if you have anything against anyone (Including yourself—I added that!) forgive him and let it drop (leave it, let it go), in order that your Father Who is in heaven may also forgive you your [own] failings and shortcomings and let them drop. But if you do not forgive, neither will your Father in heaven forgive your failings and shortcomings."

Matthew 18:21-35 (Amplified Bible)

"Then Peter came up to Him and said, Lord, how many times may my brother sin against me and I forgive him and let it go? [As many as] up to seven times? Jesus answered him, I tell you, not up to seven times, but seventy times seven! Therefore the kingdom of heaven is like a human king who wished to settle accounts with his attendants. When he began the accounting, one was brought to him who owed him 10,000 talents [probably about $10,000,000.00] And because he could not pay, his master ordered him to be sold, with his wife and his children and everything that he possessed, and payment to be made. So the attendant fell on his knees, begging him, Have patience with me and I will pay you everything. And his master's heart was moved with compassion, and he released him and forgave him [canceling] the debt. But that same attendant, as he went out, found one of his fellow attendants who owed him a hundred denarii [about twenty dollars]; and he caught him by the throat and said, Pay what you owe! So his fellow attendant fell down and begged him earnestly, Give me time, and I will pay you all! But he was unwilling and he went out and had him put in prison till he should pay the debt. When his fellow attendants saw what had happened, they were greatly distressed, and they went and told everything that had taken place to their master. Then his master called him and said to him, You contemptible and wicked attendant! I forgave and canceled all that [great] debt of yours because you begged me to. And should you not have had pity and mercy on your fellow attendant, as I had pity and mercy on you? And in wrath his master turned him over to the torturers (the jailers), till he should pay all that he owed. So also My heavenly Father will deal with every one of you if you do not freely forgive your brother from your heart his offenses."

I have tried and tried to be a better person. I have read my Bible and seen the areas in my heart that needed to be changed, and try to change them myself. One day in prayer, God showed me I was a block of wood. I know that sounds funny, and in a way it is. He's the Master Carver and I'm that block of wood. He had a plan for the wood long before the wood was even created. So, as my Loving Carver, He started to carve out the pieces that didn't belong there, to create this wonderful, beautiful figure He had planned from the beginning of time. At one point, I looked at the carving and saw it was not changing fast enough for me. I grabbed the knife from the Master Carver and tried to carve out of me what I didn't like.

In reality, this could never happen, because a block of wood cannot carve itself. God showed me what I was trying to do, the changes I was trying to make in myself, wouldn't and couldn't happen without His help. When I realized this, it freed me. It's God's job to change me by the power of His Holy Spirit, and my job is to just yield and be a piece of wood, submissive in the Master Carver's hand. I want to be carved out exactly how He wants me. He created me for a specific purpose. I know I won't be happy trying to do things my way, in my time. This helped me to just relax and trust God to strengthen me in my weaknesses (and they are many).

God has so much love for us. His love motivates Him to bring about change in our lives. His love sees our weaknesses, waits for the right time, and graciously shows us where we need to change. Our weaknesses will be removed with His love. This is awesome and gives me hope that God, with His loving touch, is at work in me to strip away the faults, wrong attitudes, negative character traits, and regrets, and replace them with His strength! As we yield, God will hold us with His loving arms. He never pushes or casts us away, only brings us near. If we press in and allow God's work to happen, we will be changed. There will be pain. Anytime we crucify our flesh there is pain involved, but the end result is awesome. We'll be more useful for His kingdom and a better person all the way around. Thank the Lord for His loving power constantly at work in all of us.

CRITICAL EYES

Throughout the history of the world, people have criticized and judged other people. The Bible tells us not to do it, and yet we do it anyway. This is sin. It was hard enough to forgive myself for my mistake, let alone think about people criticizing me for it. I understand the temptation to criticize and talk about someone. When I did find out what people were saying about me, I was crushed. It was only when I found who I was in Christ, that I could face people and walk on even in the midst of criticism. I was forgiven. God forgave me, and gave me a reason to live.

People will be critical toward us, that is a fact of life. As long as we are walking where Christ tells us to walk and doing what God tells us to do, ignore the critics. God will deal with people. He is the ultimate and only judge.

WHAT EXACTLY WAS MY FAILURE?

I pray God will heal all those involved, including the congregation I served. I haven't said exactly what sin I committed for several reasons. First, to protect all those involved. Second, if I pinpointed the sin, I believe this book would not minister to as many people. One might not relate to the exact sin and therefore, not receive what God has for them as they read this book. Third, I never want to glorify the sin, only the Forgiver of sin. Please know I generalize to protect and to minister. Truly this book is an account of God forgiving, healing, and restoring a vessel that was broken, and the steps it took to be whole again.

Chapter 7

STEP 5: DEALING WITH THE PAST
Past Effects Present

I gave my heart to Jesus at the age of nine. At the time, I didn't fully grasp why I was coming to the altar at the church my family and I attended. I went to the altar to have prayer for my home life. My stepfather was physically abusing us, and I wanted God to stop all the madness at home. After leaving the altar, I walked away with such a peace in my heart that God would help, and newness because Jesus came into my life and cleaned it all out. Remember that I was nine years old, and that's what I understood at the time. I just knew things would be better at home. Eventually my home life did get better; we left our step dad and moved into our own apartment. There were five of us now, my older sister, two younger brothers from our stepfather, and mom and I. Mom raised all of us by herself.

When I was nine, mom made me take care of my two younger brothers when she was not around. To me, it seemed like all the time. I never knew what it was like to be a little girl. Between the drunkenness and abuse of my stepfather, and taking care of my two brothers, I had to grow up fast. Throughout my life, I just wanted my real daddy to come home and be with us. "He would help us and he would be nice to us," is what I'd say to myself. He never came.

My mom and real dad were divorced when I was two years old. I never knew what it was like to have a loving father at home. At that time, all the men I knew were either abusive or neglectful. Through time, I grew to resent men. I started to rely on my mom and myself, until I asked Christ into my heart. I had to learn what it was like to be loved unconditionally by my heavenly Father.

After I grew to be an adult, I never thought I came from a hard childhood. But when I'd give my testimony or tell a friend what I experienced as a little girl, they were astonished at how I rose from the ashes. Between the physical abuse from my stepfather, growing up without my real father, taking care of my two brothers, and being molested at the age of 18, the scars I experienced affected me deeply. I took those scars into my adult life and functioned with them, and I believe part of them contributed to my failure.

My mom worked and I stayed home to take care of my brothers during the day. When she came home from work, if the house wasn't cleaned up or if something "bad" happened, I'd get in trouble. I got to the point of never telling her what really happened while she was gone. All I knew was to make sure the house was clean, my brothers were fed, and everyone was happy, then mom would be happy too, which in turn took the pressure off me. The unfortunate thing about all of it is that I carried this coping mechanism into my adult life. I always wanted to do what was right. I never wanted people to know I had flaws or that I was not "all-together." When I became a minister, I felt if people knew I was not all right, or if I had problems, they wouldn't trust me, or wouldn't want to come to me as a minister for help. I wanted to be approachable, so I never let people know I needed help or had problems. This, ultimately, was part of my downfall.

In the midst of my failure, I tried to show people that everything was all right with me. I think I was the only one who was fooled because people noticed a distance and edginess about me.

It's amazing how our past affects our present. How we were raised and the choices we've made do affect what we are today. But I tell you the truth; our past doesn't determine our future! God doesn't determine our future based upon our past!

WHO HAS NOT FAILED?

We can find examples in God's word of people who've failed and rose up to be used by God and live victorious lives. Here are several main Bible characters we all know, who've failed, but God used their lives for His glory.

Abraham's aging wife, Sarah, laughed when three men told her she would be with child in a year (Genesis 18:12 NKJV). Abraham lied about his wife being his sister to protect his own life. Yet, even with these failures, God used them to bring in a mighty nation (Genesis 12:2 NKJV). Abraham believed in the Lord. This was faith in action, and it was credited to him as righteousness (Genesis 15:6 NKJV).

Isaac was the son his parents had longed for. Truly, he shouldn't have been born to such elderly parents. He was old enough to remember that his father Abraham almost killed him with a sword. He followed in his father's footsteps and lied about his wife being his sister. Rebekah was beautiful and Isaac was afraid he would be killed and his wife taken. When he had twin boys, he favored his first-born son, Esau, which caused jealously and hatred between the two boys, and their descendants from generation to generation. Isaac was tricked by his younger son, Jacob, into giving him a blessing instead of giving it to the oldest son, Esau. Still, after all of these mistakes, Isaac truly loved God and followed after righteousness. His name is mentioned in the Bible as, "The God of Abraham, Isaac and Jacob,"[9] a covenant passed on from generation to generation.

Jacob's name means "Supplanter, or deceitful, one who takes the heel."[10] He was born holding onto his twin brother's heel. He connived with his mother, Rebekah, and stole his older brother's birthright of blessing from his father, Isaac. He was a trickster, a liar, and a deceiver. He was favored by his mother, and ultimately ran from his home to save his life from the anger of his brother, Esau. He had to work for his beautiful wife, Rachel, and was tricked into marrying her sister, Leah, too. Yet, Jacob was given a double blessing from his father Isaac (Gen. 27:27-29, 28:3-4 NKJV). Jacob wrestled with God and his name was changed to Israel. He reconciled with his brother and they forgave each other. Ultimately, Jacob was blessed everywhere he went because he followed after God. One of his sons, Joseph, became the second in command in Egypt, and saved his people from death and extinction. Jacob's descendants were as the dust of the earth, and he and his family were blessed (Genesis 28:14 NKJV).

The above paragraphs show just a few failures God used for His glory. The Bible is full of failures just like you and me. Here are a few more failures in the Bible that were used by God.

WHO	FAILURE	HOW GOD USED THEM
Moses	Murderer, struck rock to get water; disobeyed God	Faithful, freed people from Egypt & Slavery
Mirian	Jealous, Gossiped	First woman prophetess and first woman worship Leader
Noah	Drunkard	He built Ark, saved his family from the flood
Rahab	Harlot	Saved her family, also in lineage of Jesus Christ
David	Adulterer, murderer	Man after God's own heart, faithful king
Paul	Mercilessly killed Christians	Wrote 13 books of New Testament
Peter	Liar, Denied Christ	"Rock" church was built upon

Can you see yourself in any of these people? Do you know any one who might be like them? I challenge you to search your heart and see if you have any of these character traits in your life. If you do, quickly ask God for His forgiveness and receive His love to restore you.

Who has not failed? "It's not failing that's the problem; it's what one does after they've failed. To take failure as final is to be a failure. To see in failure the school of the Spirit is to let failure contribute to one's growth in Christ."[11]

If God can use these people, He can and will use you! Don't let your failure stop you from being who God created you to be. Failure is not fatal. There's life after failure. Don't listen to the lies the enemy puts in your mind; get back up and walk on after you've fallen. You can make it!

I've picked myself up many times after my failure. I wanted to give up, but had determined the Devil was a liar, and God chose me as His own. God chooses foolish things to confound the wise (I Corinthians 1:26-31 NKJV). I'm weak and foolish at times, but all the more for God to use me again for His glory! God does use weak things, you and I, for His purposes, to build His Kingdom, and to help His people.

Chapter 8

STEP 6: FINDING SELF-WORTH

Pleasing God and Not Man

When I sinned, it was hard to apply the cross of grace to my failure. My self-worth was gone and my integrity was destroyed. I wrapped my self-worth in what I did, not what Christ did for me. I felt if people approved of what I did, I was a worthwhile person, and good to have around. After destroying all I'd worked for, I felt like I was "a nobody." My self-esteem was wrapped up in the wrong source.

People will let you down. People are not always right. Even the crowd yelled, "Crucify Him!" How do you stop wanting people to approve of you? The only thing I found to stop my approval addiction from people was to long for the approval of my Heavenly Father. I'd find scripture that mentioned obeying God and read and memorize it. I'd ask God to search my heart and show me what I needed to change so my life would glorify Him. I will talk more about obedience in the next chapter, but obedience is crucial to a life of change. It was all about pleasing God and not man. It was not works, so I wouldn't boast about them, just a heart that wanted my heavenly Father pleased with me. I did feel and sense His approval.

Another thing that helped me overcome my fear of man was what Christ did for me on the cross. As I said, I was afraid of what people thought of me after my sin. I was afraid that if people even thought my name, they would think, "Kris is a sinner, she blew it. She'll never amount to anything again. All her best years are behind her." I was afraid of finger pointing and name-calling, just like in grade school; they were fears that seemed to grip my very core. How was I to show my face again in public? If I ministered again, what would people say of my past and me?

I brought this all to God in prayer and God showed me a huge, very used, wooden cross. It was stained with blood of His only Son. This cross was bigger than I was and I quickly ran behind it and hid. I could hide behind what Jesus did for me. He died for my sin. He paid the price for my failure; it was nothing I did or could ever do. That's why I could hide behind it and I wanted to hide behind it. Christ said to me, "If someone looks at you, they're looking at My cross of grace! I gave this for you; will you receive it?" My answer was quickly, "Yes! Yes, I'll receive it! Yes, I will hide behind your cross! It's bigger than my shame and sin." Soon, my self-worth was in His cross and not what I did or what people thought of me. I quickly wrote down all those thoughts and the song, "Cross of Grace," was written.

Christ took away all our transgressions on the cross; that's why we can hide behind it! It is what He did, over two thousand years ago, just for us.

Colossians 2:13-14 (NKJV) says,

"And you, being dead in your trespasses and the uncircumcision of your flesh, He has made alive together with Him, having forgiven you all trespasses, having wiped out the hand writing of requirements that was against us, which was contrary to us. And He has taken it out of the way, having nailed it to the cross."

He has taken it out of the way, for no one to see, and has nailed it to the cross, where he shed His blood for us. He alone has paid the price for all our sin. What Christ did is bigger than any wrong we've done, that's why we can hide behind what He did for us. Knowing this helped me to overcome my fear of man and place my self-worth in what Christ did for me.

CROSS OF GRACE

By Kris Belfils

I never thought I would find myself
Where I never wanted to be
The wrong I've done, the guilt and shame
It was a prison... can I be set free?

But there is a Hope! There is a cross.
There was a sacrifice for my shame.
You gave Your life, You took my place
Now I hide behind Your cross,
Your cross of grace!

I use to fear the judging eyes of man,
They knew just where I had been
I feared their words, I feared their thoughts
For my failure... was covered in my sin

My self-worth is in Your cross,
It's where I belong, I have a home.
I'm not alone, You are near

I have found my place behind Your cross of grace

Chapter 9

STEP 7: OBEDIENCE
Quick, Joyful and Total

God requires us to obey him. Just as we want our children to obey us, which pleases our hearts when they do, that's what God wants from us. We are God's children, and as His children, we need to obey our Father. This is God's will, and is easy to understand when we look at our own children.

WITHOUT COMPLAINING

It brings joy to my heart when my children obey me, especially if I don't have to remind them repeatedly. I remember one time I asked my oldest daughter to do something. At first, she did nothing. Then, with much coaching, she reluctantly started to do what I asked her to. Through it all, she complained her younger sister didn't have to do what I was asking her to do! By the time she'd finished with what I asked her, I felt as if I'd been in a wrestling match, and I'm not sure if I'd won. Did my daughter obey? Yes, she did. Did it bring joy to my heart? No, because I had to insist all along the way.

God wants us to obey without complaining and with joy! How do we do that? At first, any type of obedience is hard. Human nature says, "We want things our way in our time." When God asks us to do something our reaction is crucial to how we walk through the test. I have to say I failed the test of temptation that prompted me to write this book. Looking back, I saw God's warnings trying to help me make the right decision, but at the time, either I didn't realize the signs or I chose to ignore them, thinking I was strong and could handle it. My disobedience brought an open door to the enemy. I chose to ignore the red flags of warning, and that was a poor choice, for it lead to much death in me and those around me (See Chapter Four). Our willful disobedience affects not only ourselves, but others. This was a heavy burden I carried. I'm thankful Jesus paid the price on the cross for all my regrets.

Andrew Murray states in, *A Life Of Obedience*, "The secret of true obedience is a clear and close personal relationship to God. All our attempts to achieve full obedience will fail until we have access to His abiding fellowship. It's God's holy presence, consciously abiding with us, that keeps us from disobeying him."[12] We have to consciously stay close to God daily, or we'll slowly walk away from His direction and guidance.

I've found this out in my life and now I practice staying close to God every day. How do I do that? I spend time in prayer and study of God's word, and I keep my heart humble and moldable to Him. I always try to remember I'll self-destruct if I wander from His side. It took a while to realize this, but because of what I suffered, it has become a part of my existence. I know my weaknesses and I know Who is my strength! This is a good thing to know. This helps me to obey God quickly. He is wiser than I am, so I can trust Him.

OBEDIENCE AND SUFFERING

We learn much through suffering. Suffering is the opposite of what we want to experience. We have to surrender our will when we suffer. Our human nature wants to run from suffering. I used to run from any sign of hardship. God was often trying to show me something in the middle of my struggle, yet I tried all I could do to get out of it. Because of what I've gone through, I see the importance of experiencing the hard times, instead of trying to get out of them. It's important to obey rather than disobey. Jesus seems sweeter on the other side of a struggle or suffering than He did when just starting to walk a few steps into it. He shows us more of Himself. Jesus suffered! He suffered the cross! He suffered criticisms and people trying to kill Him, yet He obeyed and suffered for you and me. Just think, if Jesus didn't obey His Father, where would we be right now? We'd be LOST! I'm thankful for Christ's obedience and I want to show my love and thankfulness by doing what He asks of me.

OBEDIENCE BRINGS BLESSING

Jesus is the best example of a life of obedience. He obeyed and gave glory to His heavenly Father in every aspect of His life. Scripture tells us, "He grew and increased in favor of God and man" (Luke 2:52 NKJV). The definition of *favor*, in the Thorndike Barnhart Comprehensive Desk Dictionary is, "Kindness, liking; approval, condition of being liked or approved: in favor, indulgence, pardon, permission, more than fair treatment; too great kindness, gifts, or token."[13] Because of Christ's obedience, people showed Him kindness and His Heavenly Father approved of Him. People were attracted to Him. They wanted what He had. This is what we should all want for our own lives. When we obey God, God brings His favor and blessing to our lives. God's favor goes before us and opens doors.

Just as much as we enjoy our children when they obey, God enjoys our obedience. He enjoys our obedience to the point of rewarding us. I choose obedience and blessing anytime over a curse or bad consequences.

Deuteronomy 11:26 - 28 (KJV)

"Behold, I set before you this day a blessing and a curse; A blessing, if ye obey the commandments of the LORD your God, which I command you this day, and a curse, if ye will not obey the commandments of the LORD your God, but turn aside out of the way which I command you this day, to go after other gods, which ye have not known."

One of the blessings of obedience, as we have learned with Christ, is that we increase. God wants to increase or enlarge our lives. It is natural to increase.

Psalm 115:12-15 (NKJV)

"The LORD has been mindful of us; He will bless us; He will bless the house of Israel; He will bless the house of Aaron. He will bless those who fear the LORD both small and great. May the LORD give you increase more and more, You and your children. May you be blessed by the LORD, who made heaven and earth."

Psalm 119:32 (NKJV)
"I will run the course of Your commandments, For You shall enlarge my heart."

We all have self-will. We can decide to obey or disobey. Disobedience is a form of rebellion. You are saying in essence, "I will do this my way. I don't have to listen to you." In reality, if we don't obey God, we are saying to God and everyone else that we are wiser. This is a form of pride. Disobedience opens the door to the enemy and allows him to have more control over us. Obedience closes that door and opens the best door to God's blessings. The more we obey God, even in the small things, the more God will use us and entrust us to do more. The less we obey God, especially in the small things, the less God will use us and, instead, take away things to bring us to a place of humbleness. He did it with the Israelites, and He will do it with us.

OBEDIENCE AND THE PROMISED LAND

The Children of Israel complained in the wilderness over so many things. They complained about their food, their water, the weather, other nations, and even themselves. They complained so much, it began to warp their view of freedom, and soon, they wanted to go back to Egypt, back to slavery. Did God bless them? Did He give them what they wanted? On occasion God gave them what they wanted, but for the most part, He never gave them what He promised until the old generation had passed away. God waited until all the complainers were gone. Forty years later they were ready to possess the Promised Land. God gave them many commands to obey to possess the Promised Land, and if they didn't obey those commands, He wouldn't bless them.

Deuteronomy 4:1 (Amplified Bible)
"Now listen and give heed, O Israel, to the statutes and ordinances

which I teach you, and do them, that you may live and go in and possess the land which the Lord, the God of your Fathers, gives you."

"...Give heed and do them..." is the key to this scripture. We are to look, to listen, and do what God has commanded us to do. God commanded the Israelites to do many things; here are the basics.

10 COMMANDMENTS
Deuteronomy 5:7-21

1. You shall have no other gods before Me.
2. You shall not make a carved image, not bow down to it, nor serve it.
3. You shall not take the name of the LORD your God in vain.
4. Observe the Sabbath day, to keep it holy.
5. Honor your father and your mother.
6. You shall not murder.
7. You shall not commit adultery.
8. You shall not steal.
9. You shall not bear false witness against your neighbor.
10. You shall not covet.

Along with the Ten Commandments, God gave them guidelines for worship and everyday life.

Deuteronomy 6:5-9 (NKJV)
"You shall love the LORD your God with all your heart, with all your soul, and with all your strength. And these words which I command you today shall be in your heart. You shall teach them diligently to your children, and shall talk of them when you sit in your house, when you walk by the way, when you lie down, and when you rise up. You shall bind them as a sign on your hand, and they shall be as frontlets between your eyes. You shall write them on the doorposts of your house and on your gates."

God wanted the Israelites to get these commands in their hearts, to live them and pass them on to their children. God didn't give these commands to bring hardship, but to help the Israelites have healthy guidelines to live their lives by. By following them, they would live long lives and be blessed by God.

We can surely learn from the actions of the Israelites. When they obeyed, they were blessed, but when they disobeyed, they didn't receive a blessing, only correction, chastening and even punishment. The LORD gave them many warnings to obey or He would correct them. He made it very clear what He wanted His people to do. Also, through Moses, God spoke of what would happen if the people felt they gained the Promised Land by their own strength.

Deuteronomy 8:11-20 (NKJV - Moses is speaking)

"Beware that you do not forget the LORD your God by not keeping His commandments, His judgments, and His statutes which I command you today, test—when you have eaten and are full, and have built beautiful houses and dwell in them; and when your herds and your flocks multiply, and your silver and your gold are multiplied, and all that you have is multiplied; when your heart is lifted up and you forget the LORD your God who brought you out of the land of Egypt, from the house of bondage; who led you through the great and terrible wilderness, in which were fiery serpents and scorpions and thirsty land where there was no water; who brought water for you out of the flinty rock; who fed you in the wilderness with manna, which your fathers did not know, that He might humble you and that He might test you, to do you good in the end- then you say in your heart, My power and the might of my hand have gained me this wealth. And you shall remember the Lord your God, for it is He who gives you power to get wealth, that He may establish His covenant which He swore to your fathers, as it is this day. Then it shall be, if you by any means forget the LORD your God, and follow other gods, and serve them and worship them, I testify against you this day that you shall surely perish. As the nations which the LORD destroys before you, so you shall perish, because you would not be obedient to the voice of the LORD your God."

Here is a simple reminder of the above passage that I printed out and placed in my bedroom to help me stay close to God. You might think this is really simple, but as we live our lives from day to day, we can slowly walk away from these guidelines and stray from the destiny God has chosen for us.

QUICK STEPS TO STAY CLOSE TO GOD

1. Love the Lord your God.
2. Obey God's commands and statutes.
3. Serve God with all your heart and soul, your very strength.
4. Hold fast to God.
5. Walk in God's ways, always.
6. Serve no other gods
7. Follow and obey, even when it hurts.

It is easy for our flesh to get in the way of what God did and take credit for it. We have to be on the alert of this. Don't glory in your own accomplishments, when God is the one who brought them in your life. God promised me a Promised Land if I would follow His commands. Somewhere along the way, I started doing my own thing and eventually I strayed from what God wanted for me.

I did a study on the Promised Land inhabitants, those who lived there before the Israelites came and possessed it. I found out some interesting information. The Bible states that the Canaanites, Hittites, Hivites, Perizzites, Girgashites, and the Jebusites lived in the Promised Land (Joshua 3:10-11, KJV). These were the first seven mightier nations dispossessed of their lands by the Israelites and Joshua.

Okay, put on your thinking caps as I translate their names from the originally Hebrew. Canaanites is translated, "zealous, a merchant, or trader."[14] It is partially from Kenaan, which means "lowland."[15] Kenaan is the fourth son of Ham. Kenaan is partially from Kana, which means, "to be humbled, be humbled, be subdued, be brought down, be low, be under, be brought into subjection, to humble oneself."[16]

Hittites is translated, "descendant of Heth."[17] Hittite is related to Heth, or "terror,"[18] and is a form of chathath which means, "To be shattered, be dismayed, be broken, be abolished, be afraid, to cause to be dismayed or terrify."[19] Hivites is translated "villagers."[20] A possible related word is chavvah, which means, "village, town, tent village, also life-giving, living place."[21]

Perizzites is translated "belonging to a village."[22] Perizzite is also a form of peraziy or peroziy, which means, "villager, rural dweller, hamlet-dweller."[23] Another related word is perazah meaning, "open region, un-walled village, open country,"[24] and also related is paraz from an unused root meaning "to separate, i.e. to decide."[25]

Girgashites is translated "dwelling on a clayey soil."[26]

Amorites is translated as "a sayer."[27] A related word is amar, or "to say, speak, or utter, to say, to answer, to say in one's heart, to think, to command, to promise, to intend, to be told, to be said, to be called, to boast, to act proudly."[28]

Jebusites is translated as "inhabitant of Jebus."[29] A related word is Jebus or "Descendants of Jebus."[30] Jebus also means threshing place." A related word is bus, or "to tread down, reject, trample down, rejection."[31]

First Seven Nations Conquered by Joshua

Canaanites—zealous, "to be humbled," Canaan = "lowland"

Hittites—"To be dismayed, shattered, broken, be afraid, terrorized"

Hivites—"Villagers, town, tent-dwelling, lifegiving, living place"

Perizzites—Belonging to a village, rural dweller, open region, un-walled, to separate"

Girgashites—"dwelling on a clayey soil"

Amorites—"a sayer; to say, speak, say in one's heart, think, boast or act proudly"

Jebusites—"To trod down, reject, trample down to kick out to be trodden down."

The meanings of the names of those who occupied the Promised Land before the Israelites came and possessed it were exactly the issues in my heart that God was healing me of. My self-esteem was extremely low. I was living in the "lowlands," (Canaanites), thinking I was a loser and wanting to end my life. I was afraid, shattered and even broken (Hittites). I was afraid to see people who knew of my failure and possibly be quick to judge me. I was shattered of all that I had worked for and the Kris I used to know. Broken! I was fully and completely broken of my self-will. My pride was gone. God's refining fire brought this change and correction in my life. Before my failure, I would boast (Amorites) in my heart, and to others, of how God used me. People would praise me for my sermons or worship leading and I'd take it to heart instead of laying those crowns at the feet of Jesus. People would tell me how they enjoyed my sermons and preaching style, and that they could understand and apply my sermons better, as compared to the senior pastor. Pride (Amorites) began to well up inside me. The next thing I knew, I was falling into sin with my pride leading the way (Proverbs 16:18). I was rejected (Jebusites) and stripped of so many things. I was trodden down and trampled by the enemy and even myself. I was my worst enemy. My heart was hardened before the failure, but after it, through God's refining fire, it became soft and clay like again (Girgashites).

You might say, "You're reaching, Kris, trying to connect the nations that were destroyed, with your life." Truly, there's a direct correlation. God had to bring me to this place in my life to dispossess all that I had mentioned, utterly destroy it so I would be ready to possess the promised land He offered me. Pride had to go! My heart had to be softened. I needed to be humbled and broken. I had to get to a place where I relied solely upon God and not my abilities or work.

Has God offered you a Promised Land? What areas in your life is He dealing with to prepare you to possess your Promised Land? Do any of the nations' names, which had lived in the Promised Land before the Israelites conquered it, mean anything to you?

God has a unique plan for all of us. We were all created to do certain works. The soil of our heart can get very hardened. Allow God to soften your heart. Have a heart of obedience. It will cost you something for sure, but its well worth the cost and the wait to obtain that Promised Land that awaits you! Obedience brings God's favor (blessing) upon your life.

I wanted to write a song about obeying God and in that obedience, laying down my life and crowns. I realized I wanted God more than I wanted my way or my desires. I never wanted to long for or pursue my desires and dreams over my relationship with my God.

As we lay down our crowns and dreams, God has freedom to lead us to our destiny.

LISTEN AND OBEY

By Kris Belfils

I'll obey You Lord
With all my heart
I will serve You
All of my days

I am here and I come
I lay my life down
I lay down my crown
And I know You are here with me
Hold me close and never let me go

As You lead me I will follow
Wash me clean I pray
Speak to me, take me deeper in You
I will listen and obey
I will listen and obey

Chapter 10

STEP 8: FINDING ENCOURAGEMENT
Help from the Psalms

During my refining fire season, I embraced many passages of scripture that helped me heal and walk on.

The biggest help was from the book of Psalms. It was my portion to live on each day. I'd read it in the morning and again at night.

I'd even place the Bible on my head at times asking God to help get His word in my mind and heart. I remember pointing out verses to God and saying, "These are Your words! You promised them to everyone and that includes me. Please help me to get them in my spirit."

I know God loved me through those tough days right after coming home from the hospital. Much mercy and grace was given to me in those times of need. I'd cry out to God for help, and soon I felt peace.

My circumstances didn't change, but I was at peace as long as I kept my eyes on God. The moments of peace grew and soon they would fill my whole day. It took time for this to happen.

In the meantime, the only thing I could do was to cry out to God and read His words of comfort. Here are just a few of the verses in the Psalms that really comforted me and I pray they comfort and encourage you as well.

HELP FROM THE PSALMS

1. God Is a Shield and the Lifter of My Head.

Psalm 3:2-5 (NKJV)

"Many are they who say of me, 'There is no help for him in God.' But You, O LORD, are a shield for me, my glory and the One who lifts up my head. I cried to the LORD with my voice, And He heard me from His holy hill. I lay down and slept; I awoke, for the LORD sustained me."

2. God Lifts Me from the Gates of Death (Even by My Own Hand).

Psalm 9:12b-14 (NKJV)

"...He does not forget the cry of the humble (afflicted), Have mercy on me, O LORD! Consider my trouble from those who hate me, You who lift me up from the gates of death, That I may tell of all Your praise in the gates of the daughter of Zion. I will rejoice in Your salvation."

I have to pause here and expand on these verses for just a moment. Here it states that God "lifts me up from the gates of death." God rescued me from my attempt to kill myself. He lifted me up from the very gates I was headed for. Satan wanted me destroyed and I was falling right into his plan, but God had a better plan. He reached down in the midst of my mess and picked me up and said, "Enough! I won't allow this to happen, for I have a plan for your life!" This is God's mercy, love and character to lift me up even after I'd sinned and made a mess of my life. He will not allow his children to be destroyed. Even in the middle of bad choices and self-destruction, God said, "No!" Aren't you glad God follows His plan instead of ours? He loves us and He is faithful even when we are not. In the midst of my unfaithfulness, God loved me and rescued me from me. This is His incredible love and grace.

"That I may tell of all Your praise in the gates of the daughter of Zion. I will rejoice in Your salvation." There are two gates this passage of scripture is referring to; the gates of death and the gates of the daughters of Zion (Jerusalem). Both give entrance or exit to a place. Here, God rescued me from the gates of death and allowed me to walk in through the gates of the daughters of Zion. The gate of a city, in the Bible, was often a public place. It was a place of meeting to buy and sell, or a place where the courts of justice were held. It was a "public presence" place (KJV).[32] Not only did God rescue me from death, but also He put me in a place of life. He not only saved me from me, He restored me back to a living, breathing, healthy person again. This is how God works. He is for us, always. This brings joy and causes me to rejoice. He is for us and never against us.

3. God Shows Me the Path for My Life.

Psalm 16:11 (NKJV)
"You will show me the path of life; In Your presence is fullness of joy; At Your right hand are pleasures forevermore."

4. God Hears My Calls of Distress.

Psalm 18:4-6 (NKJV)
"The pangs of death surrounded me, and the floods of ungodliness made me afraid. The sorrows of Sheol surrounded me; The snares of death confronted me. In my distress I called upon the LORD, and cried out to my God; He heard my voice from His temple, and my cry came before Him, even to His ears."

This passage of scripture ministered to me immensely. "The pangs of death surrounded me..." This is where I was after trying to kill myself. I still had to find a reason why I wanted to keep living. Yes, I was glad I didn't die, but my old way of thinking about myself was still there. I had a negative self-image. "The floods of ungodliness made me afraid." This was my own sin and bad choices, which was ungodliness, which led up to wanting my life to end. "The sorrows of Sheol or Hell surrounded me; the snares of death confronted me." I was right at the brink of death. At the time, it was what I wanted, but looking back, I never want to be there again. I can still taste the affects of those choices today. Despair and loneliness surrounded me. Everything seemed dark and hopeless. "In my distress I called upon the LORD, and cried out to my God; He heard my voice from His temple, and my cry came before Him, even to His ears." God heard my cries for help. He wanted me to get to a place of total need for Him. When I cried out to Him, He came and delivered me. Often God brings us to a place that we see our need for Him. At this place, our self-sufficiency dies and we learn to trust God for our lives.

5. God Cleanses Me from Secret Faults and Keeps Me from Making the Same Mistakes.

Psalm 19:12-13 (NKJV)

"Who can understand his errors? Cleanse me from secret faults. Keep back Your servant also from presumptuous sins; let them not have dominion over me. Then I shall be blameless, and I shall be innocent of great transgression."

God is the only One who can cleanse us from our secret faults and sins. Anything that we do in secret, what we may hide from our boss, friends and family, or anyone who might be looking, is wrong and we are walking in the flesh. Let this be a sign for you. If you have to hide it, don't do it.

6. God Is My Shepherd and He Makes Me Rest.

I have read Psalm 23 many times in my life, but during this time, the words seemed to jump out of the page and wrapped itself around me like a warm, friendly blanket. Each verse of Psalm 23 had new meaning.

Psalm 23:1 (Amplified Bible)

"The LORD is my Shepherd [to feed, guide, and shield me], I shall not lack."

All our desires and frustrations are nothing compared to our loving Shepherd. He is all we need. All our anxieties and regrets; God is bigger! All our shame and all the things we may have lost are shadows compared to His glory.

I finally saw God instead of people, position, and possessions. My Shepherd was more than enough for me. I could see myself letting go of all I treasured and watching them all fall like sand through my fingers. When all had fallen, I reached out for my Good Shepherd and He reached for me and brought comfort.

Psalm 23:2 (Amplified Bible)
"He makes me lie down in [fresh, tender] green pastures; He leads me beside the still and restful waters."

This verse is powerful. "He makes me lie down..." It doesn't say, "He asks me," or "He suggests that I lie down." God makes us lie down in green pastures when we really need to rest, even when we don't think we need to. I needed to rest, and didn't even realize it. God required rest. I'm a go, go, go person. I was driven. I was a NOW woman. God wanted me to rest even when I didn't want to. God brought me to green pastures to lie down in them. Not to just stand by them or to sit in them, but to totally lie in them and experience them. Green pastures, or tender, green, long grass is really heaven on earth for sheep. We are His sheep, and resting in long green grass is exactly what we need to get totally nourished and healthy again. Thank God for His tender green grass which He makes us lie in! For me, this was a "time out" period of reading, and learning more about God, a time to heal and take care of myself. During prayer one morning, God gave me a vision. In this vision, I was walking along a path. The only thing I could see was my feet. Along side of me was Jesus walking with me. Still, I could only see Jesus and my feet. I could hear the crunch of the rocks under our feet as we walked. Jesus didn't walk in front of me, or behind me, but right along side of me. As we walked, our cadence was exactly the same. We walked and walked and then the path opened up to the left of us into this beautiful meadow of long green grass. The meadow sloped down to a quiet still lake of water. On the other side of the lake was a huge rock several stories high. Jesus brought me to the green grass and motioned for me to sit down beside Him. As we sat together, He pointed to the grass and showed me how long and green it was. Then He motioned to the water and showed me several fish swimming in the clear still lake. He looked across the water to the big rock and showed me the majestic structure of it. I would look where He was pointing, and then quickly bring my gaze back on His face and intently look in His eyes. I couldn't help it. He captivated my attention. He was so beautiful and gentle. He took His time with me, sharing every little thing in this quiet place of rest. I could have stayed there forever with Him. Every once in a while, I would think, "What is down the path from here?" Then, I would quickly focus on Jesus again. Down the path would come later in my life. This was exactly where I was supposed to be, resting, learning, and sitting with Christ.

The latter part of Psalm 23:2 is connected with the beginning of verse two, for without times of drinking His still and restful waters, we would not be truly nourished and ready again to travel where the Shepherd guides us. His waters are still, quiet, and restful. They are rich and taste wonderful. He leads us to those waters. He wants us there. We need to be there. Don't fight it when God makes you lie down in green pastures and when He leads you beside those quiet, still waters of refreshment. You will walk away from those times filled and overflowing with His love and goodness, if you'll allow yourself to rest and drink.

Psalm 23:3 (Amplified)
"He refreshes and restores my life (my self); He leads me in the paths of righteousness [uprightness and right standing with Him—not for my earning it, but] for His name's sake."

"He refreshes and restores my life (my self)..." This is an offshoot of the above verse and the outcome of resting and lying down in green pastures and still waters. It's a blessing from God. God is for us! I can't say it enough in this book. I think some Christians believe God is not always for us, but is only a God of judgment. Yet, the reality of how much God does love us and how much He wants to see us succeed is huge.

Do you need refreshing and restoring? Submit to God's time frame and rest and be refreshed. No one can take care of you but you! You are the one who needs to stop and smell the roses. A better way to say it is, "O taste and see that the LORD is good: blessed is the man that trusts in Him" (Psalm 34:8).

"He leads me in the paths of righteousness..." Aren't you thankful God leads us in paths of righteousness? As we submit our lives to God, He takes over and leads us on right paths for His name's sake and for His glory! It takes the pressure off us. Yes, we need to walk in the spirit and not the flesh, but it is such an assurance that God is our shepherd leading us every step of the way, especially through the narrow and rocky paths.

Psalm 23:4 (Amplified Bible)
"Yes, though I walk through the [deep, sunless] valley of the shadow of death, I will fear or dread no evil, for You are with me; Your rod [to protect] and Your staff [to guide], they comfort me."

We will walk through dark, sunless valleys in our lifetime. I did, and I made it through, and you can too! During my dark valley, I read this Psalm over and over again. It ministered to me, especially the part of walking through the dark valley of death. Satan wanted me dead! He almost won. With my own hands, I tried to kill myself, thinking there was no hope. It was a dark and lonely place. But, only God! God was there and walked through it with me and rescued me. After leaving the hospital after my suicide attempt, I was still in a dark valley. It took some time for me to walk through it. Days, weeks and even months went by just trying to function in this dark place, but the difference was surrendering my life to Christ totally and completely. When I gave up control, the darkness lifted a great deal.

God can and will walk with us in our dark times of emotional stress, spiritual lack, physical pain and ailments, financial loss and even mental breakdowns. He is our Good Shepherd leading us with His rod of protection and His staff of guidance. In Hebrew, rod is shay'-bet, or (literally) "a stick for punishing, writing, fighting, ruling, walking."[33] God uses His rod of correction just like a shepherd would on a sheep that's straying or is strong-willed. He will correct us and bring us back on the right path for His name's sake. The Hebrew word for staff is mish-ay-naw' or mish-eh'-neth which means, "support, sustenance, or walking stick."[34] With one stick our Good Shepherd corrects us and with the other He supports, or comforts us. Comforts in the Hebrew is naw-kham' or "sighs, or breaths strongly, pity or console."[35] This is awesome that God pities or consoles us. We are never alone! God is always there to help us.

Psalm 23:5 (Amplified Bible)
"You prepare a table before me in the presence of my enemies. You anoint my head with oil; my [brimming] cup runs over."

God will bring times of feasting and celebration right in front of our enemies. He will also allow our enemies to see the blessings God has given us as we walk in His ways. Not for something that we've done, but because of whom Jesus Christ is!

"You anoint my head with oil; my cup runs over." This refreshes and anoints. In hot climates oil was applied to people to help with the heat. It refreshed them and usually there was some type of perfume in the oil that would give off a wonderful scent. Here, God anoints His sheep with oil that would help with the heat and insects and it also shows richness and fruitfulness.

"My cup runs over..." expresses that we lack nothing; in fact we have more than we can contain. We will always be totally satisfied when we make the Lord our Shepherd and let Him protect and guide us.

Psalm 23:6 (Amplified Bible)
"Surely or only goodness, mercy, and unfailing love shall follow me all the days of my life, and through the length of my days the house of the Lord [and His presence] shall be my dwelling place."

"Surely goodness, mercy, and unfailing love shall follow me all the days of my life..." How awesome is that? Imagine that mercy, goodness, and love are people who follow you everywhere you go. They are there when you lie down to sleep. When you get up in the morning, they are there waiting to help and support you. They are always there for your good. God has so much goodness to give us. His mercies are new every morning, great is His faithfulness (Lamentations 3:22 & 23). We shall dwell with Him in His house forever, constantly being in His presence, which we can experience here on earth too.

There's so much more we could talk about on Psalm 23. Read it for yourself, and listen to what God tells you about your situation. He is our good shepherd!

7. God Strengthens Me as I Wait for Him.

Psalm 27:14 (NKJV)
"Wait on the LORD; Be of good courage, and He shall strengthen your heart; Wait, I say, on the LORD!"

Psalm 31:24 (NKJV)
"Be of good courage, and He shall strengthen your heart, all you who hope (wait) in the LORD."

It's hard to wait on God. Actually, if you are like me, it's hard to wait for anything. But, these verses encourage us to wait on God and when we wait, God will strengthen our hearts. God is at work in our lives. When we wait, we should learn to wait with joy and expectation. If God has promised you something, or you are believing God to do something, rest in the knowledge that God has ordained this waiting time for you. During this time, God will show you areas in your life He wants you to look at and notice. These areas can be big or small. Are you willing to allow God to bring change in the areas He has already shown you? I encourage you to yield to His loving hand and release them to Him. To make the waiting time the most productive, release those attitudes, feelings, reactions, or anything God is requiring in your life, and He will help you overcome them. God wouldn't bring your attention to them and not help you with them. He loves you and wants the very best to come out. He created you, and knows how you function and think. Knowing this helps you to release them and allow God to heal you and change you. It is a process. It does take time. What better way to help the waiting time go faster then to do something while you're waiting. Allow God to smooth your rough edges with His loving sandpaper.

8. Hope in God and He Will Help.

Psalm 42:11 (NKJV)
"Why are you cast down, O my soul? And why are you disquieted

within me? Hope in God; For I shall yet praise Him, The help (salvation) of my countenance and my God."

(The Message Bible)

"Why are you down in the dumps, dear soul? Why are you crying the blues? Fix my eyes on God-soon I'll be praising again. He puts a smile on my face. He's my God."

This verse is one I look at constantly. When I feel lonely or depressed, I look at this verse and it reminds me that to keep my eyes on God rather than on my life and my problems. When we keep our focus on Christ, the things of the world are not overwhelming. The moment we turn our eyes from Him and look at ourselves, we will start to sink under the waves. Peter found this out when he walked on water to Jesus, and sank when he looked at the wind and the waves (Matthew 14:28-32). When Christ is our focus, we will succeed.

9. God Shows Mercy, Cleanses, Purges, and Restores Me.

Psalm 51:1-17 (NKJV)

"Have mercy upon me, O God, according to Your loving kindness; according to the multitude of Your tender mercies, blot out my transgressions. Wash me thoroughly from my iniquity, and cleanse me from my sin. For I acknowledge my transgressions, and my sin is always before me. Against You, You only, have I sinned, and done this evil in Your sight—that You may be found just when You speak, and blameless when You judge. Behold, I was brought forth in iniquity, and in sin my mother conceived me. Behold, You desire truth in the inward parts, and in the hidden part You will make me to know wisdom. Purge me with hyssop, and I shall be clean; wash me, and I shall be whiter than snow. Make me hear joy and gladness, that the bones You have broken may rejoice. Hide Your face from my sins, and blot out all my iniquities. Create in me a clean heart, O God, and renew a steadfast spirit within me. Do not cast me away from Your presence, and do not take Your Holy Spirit from me. Restore to me the joy of Your salvation, and uphold me by Your generous Spirit. Then I will teach transgressors Your ways, and sinners shall be converted to You. Deliver me from the guilt of bloodshed, O God, the God of my salvation, and my tongue shall sing aloud of Your righteousness. O Lord, open my lips, and my mouth shall show forth Your praise. For You do not desire sacrifice, or else I would give it; You do not delight in burnt offering. The sacrifices of God are a broken spirit, a broken and contrite heart—these, O God, You will not despise."

This passage is very real to me. It was as if David wrote it from my heart. I need God's mercy desperately! Once we go to God and confess our sins, and truly repent, God always accepts us and covers us with His mercy and grace. He doesn't like the sin, but He does love the sinner-- you and me. After my transgression, I would go to God often and confess to Him how I felt, what happened, what I did, and ask Him what I needed to do. He's my best friend. I can tell God anything and He will not turn me away.

Note David asks God to cleanse, purge and then restore him. There is a process God must take all of us through after we have sinned. God will cleanse us after we've sinned, all we have to do ask Him. We need God's purging to burn out all the impurities that are in our hearts, like pride, selfishness, bad attitudes, lack of self-control, and much more. These are works of the flesh (Galatians 5:19-21). They are deep issues that take time to burn out and heal. God will restore us to be even stronger. Psalm 66:10-12 (NKJV) states, "For You, O God, have tested us; You have refined us as silver is refined. You brought us into the net; You laid affliction on our backs. You have caused men to ride over our heads; we went through fire and through water; but you brought us out to rich fulfillment." Allow God to burn out all the dross in your life. The fire might seem hot, but the end results are worth the perseverance in the heat.

David also pleaded to God to not cast him away from His presence or take His Holy Spirit from him. I believe David truly knew and tasted the joy of being in God's presence and pleasing Him. David also knew and felt God's precious Holy Spirit. I can't imagine going through life without God and His presence, but that's what we do when we start making wrong choices that separate us from God.

I'm sure you've heard the phrase, "The Devil made me do it." The Bible says, "...Walk in the Spirit and you shall not fulfill the lust of the flesh" (Galatians 5:16). It's our choice. David knew he was the one who lay with Bathsheba and had sex with her and then killed her husband by placing him in battle. Psalm 51 shows how David felt and responded after Nathan, the prophet, came to him and confronted him on the issue. God restored David after he repented and followed God.

One more thing I want to mention concerning Psalms 51 is verses 15 and 16 (NKJV). "For you do not desire sacrifice, or else I would give it; you do not delight in burnt offering. The sacrifices of God are a broken spirit, a broken and contrite heart—these, O God, You will not despise." This statement was said during the time God did delight in sacrifices. The only way to come to God was through the various sacrifices each person had to bring to the priests for forgiveness. That's what God taught the Israelites through Moses and it was carried down and practiced during King David's day as well. But these verses clearly state God doesn't delight in sacrifices or burnt offerings. What God does delight in is a broken spirit, where pride and our will is broken. A broken and contrite heart, God will never despise. The Barbour Student Bible Dictionary states the meaning for despise is "Detest, loath, reject, scorn, to look down upon."[36] God will never look down upon our broken, contrite heart and spirit. This, above all other sacrifices, God will always receive. I have found that God will bring us to a place of brokenness to humble us and to show us we need Him. This is what happened to David, this is what happened to me, and I am sure it will happen to you if it hasn't already. I want to please God and constantly allow Him to have control of my life. It is too much work to walk through another humbling experience like I walked through after my failure, yet I am thankful for where I'm at in Christ today because of the processes God walked me through.

10. When I Wait in Silence, God Brings His Salvation and Defense.

Psalm 62:1-2 (NKJV)

"Truly my soul silently waits for God; from Him comes my salvation. He only is my rock and my salvation; He is my defense; I shall not be greatly moved."

It's hard to wait for anything, let alone wait for God. But, place on top of it the need for God to defend you in trouble, and it can seem almost endless. This verse states, "... my soul silently waits..." Silently is without complaint. Silently is without question. Silently means to not speak. It's trusting that God will come and help, no matter how long it takes. Waiting for God to rise up and defend us is a hard wait indeed.

Many times I wanted to rise up and be my own defense and tell people my side of the story, but I couldn't. Many times people would hear from other sources of the sin I'd committed. I had no way of being vindicated. I had no way of telling my side of what happened. I was a sinner. I couldn't deny it. I had to rely on God to be my defense. When God is our defense we are defended completely. If I could rise up and tell the world my side, it would come across in a bad way. It would be like someone trying to tell others about their own gifts and talents and bragging about them. It leaves the listener feeling kind of sick and it makes one look prideful.

God showed me this about wanting to be vindicated. He said to me, "I'm your defense," and I needed no other. He's the best defense attorney we could ever have. So I silently waited for God to come and defend me and to uphold me. This brought a trust factor I never thought was possible.

Chapter II

STEP 9: LEARNING HOW TO TRUST GOD

Trust Factor

Charles H. Spurgeon said in a sermon on personal service, "Trust Jesus, and you are saved. Trust self, and you are lost."[37] That's a profound statement, and so true. If we trust ourselves, we can lead ourselves astray. Our human nature wants to rely on our self. After all, we're always there, always looking out for number one, and we think we know what's best for us. Unfortunately we don't see the whole picture to really make the best decisions. God sees everything. He knows all about you and your character. He knows you better than you know yourself. He created you! Therefore, the Creator knows more about His creation then that creation knows about itself. God created you for a specific purpose and plan. He "knit you in your mother's womb," (Psalm 139:13 Amplified Bible) and you're "fearfully and wonderfully made" (Psalms 139:14 NKJV). He knows you. He knows how you will respond or not respond to things. It's wise to trust the Creator of our lives for everything. For what He created is wonderful and marvelous, and our soul knows very well (Psalm 139:14b NKJV).

Trust is faith in action. It believes God is working on your situation. Even though we don't know just how God is working, He is! Even if we can't see Him working at the start, He is! Our eyes and understanding are limited. When we don't see the results we want, our faith falters, and we are left with worry and doubt. I know, I've done it many times. But, in those moments of looking and not seeing, tell yourself, "Hold on!" Say out loud, "I can trust Him!" I know I've said this earlier, but I have to say it again, "When you don't see God's hand working out your troubles, trust His heart." His heart is for you! He's making a way where there seems to be no way. He's restoring you. He's working out your situation for His glory and in His time.

God wants us to trust Him with all things. How do we do that? If we do trust God, will He make us do something we don't want to do? Would He change us into something we don't want to be if we give Him total and complete control? It's hard to trust until we read more about why we should trust.

The trust issue in my life was big. I fought and struggled with it. I was reading in the Psalms and noticed so many passages that mentioned trust and what happens when I do trust Him. I found over eighty-five verses between NKJV and CEV that talk about trusting God and what the results will be. In the Contemporary English Version, the word, "trust" is translated as "wait", "hope", "believe" or "steadfastness". They seemed to be interchangeable; also "love" and "mercy" are interchangeable as well. Knowing the facts about trusting God helps us to trust Him.

TRUST FACTOR
From the Book of Psalms

VRS	TRANS	TRUST FACTOR	RESULTS
2:12b	NKJV	Blessed are those who put their trust in Him	Blessing/favor
4:5	NKJV/CEV	Offer the sacrifices of righteousness and trust	Obedience/favor
5:11,12	NKJV	Let all those rejoice who put their trust	Joy, defense, favor
7:1	NKJV	O LORD my God, in You I put my trust	Safety, deliverance
9:10	CEV/NKJV	Everyone who honors Your name can trust You	God is faithful
11:1	NKJV	In the Lord I put my trust	Surety
13:5	NKJV	I trusted in Your mercy	Forgiveness, salvation
16:1	NKJV	In You I put my trust	Preserves me
17:7	NKJV	O You who save those who trust in You	Salvation/rescues
18:2	NKJV	My God, my strength, in whom I will trust	Rock, fortress, deliverer

18:30	NKJV	He is a shield to all who trust in Him	Shield, protector
20:7	CEV/NKJV	Some trust the power of chariots or horses	We trust You, surety
21:7	NKJV	For the king trusts in the LORD	Shall not be moved
22:4	NKJV	Our father's trusted in You	Deliverance
22:5	NKJV	They trust in You	They were not ashamed
22:8	NKJV/CEV	He trusted in the LORD	Rescue, deliver
22:9	NKJV	You made Me trust (Jesus speaking)	God helps us to trust
25:2	NKJV/CEV	O my God, I trust in You	Not ashamed, not defeated
25:5	CEV	I always trust You	Guide, instruct, safety
25:20	NKJV	I put my trust in You	Keeps, delivers, no shame
25:21	CEV/NKJV	I trust You	Integrity and uprightness
26:1	NKJV	I have also trusted in the LORD	Vindicates, shall not slip
27:3	CEV	I will trust You	No fear in the face of war
27:14	CEV	Trust the LORD!	Strength and bravery
28:7	CEV/NKJV	I trust you completely.	Strong shield, help
31:1	NKJV	In You, O LORD, I put my trust	Never ashamed, deliverer
31:5	CEV	I trust You	Faithful, rescued me
31:6, 7	NKJV/CEV	But, I trust in the LORD	Glad, Rejoice in mercy
31:14	CEV/NKJV	I trust You, LORD	I claim you as my God
31:19	CEV/NKJV	For all who honor and trust You	Blessings stored up for us
31:24	CEV	All who trust the LORD	Cheerful and strong
32:10	NKJV/CEV	He who trusts in the LORD	Mercy surrounds, gladness
33:18	CEV	Honor and trust His kindness	LORD watches over
33:21	NKJV/CEV	We have trusted in His holy name	Hearts rejoice
34:8	NKJV	Blessed is the man who trusts in Him	Blessed, God is good
34:10	CEV	But if you trust the LORD	Never miss anything good
34:22	NKJV	Those who trust in Him	Never condemned, saved

36:7, 8	NKJV	Children of men put their trust	Lovingkindness, satisfied
37:3	NKJV/CEV	Trust in the LORD and live right	Desires of heart
37:5	CEV	Trust Him to help	God will lead you
37:7, 9	CEV	Trust the LORD	The land will be yours
37:34	CEV	Trust the LORD and follow Him	Land, wicked destroyed
38:15	CEV	I trust You, LORD God	He will do something
40:3	CEV/NKJV	They will honor and trust You	New song, blessing
40:4	NKJV/CEV	Blessed is that man that makes the Lord his trust	Blessed
42:5, 11	CEV	I trust You!	God removes depression
43:5	CEV	I trust You!	Not discouraged/ restless
52:8	NKJV	I trust in the mercy of God forever and ever	Like a green olive tree
55:23	NKJV/CEV	But I will trust in You.	Destruction to evil men
56:3	NKJV	I will trust in You	Whenever I am afraid
56:4	NKJV/CEV	In God I have put my trust	No fear, safety
56:11	CEV/NKJV	I trust You	No fear, no harm
57:1	NKJV	For my soul trusts in You	Mercy, refuge
61:4	NKJV	I will trust in the shelter of Your wings	Fellowship, shelter
62:8	CEV/NKJV	Trust God	Tell Him your concerns
64:10	NKJV	Be glad in the LORD, and trust in Him	Gladness, shall glory
71:1	NKJV	In You, O LORD, I put my trust	Never be ashamed
71:5	NKJV	You are my trust from my youth	Hope
73:28	NKJV	I have put my trust in the Lord God	Draw close/declare works
78:7	CEV	Then they would trust God and obey	Remember what God did
78:22	CEV	They had refused to trust Him	No salvation
84:12	NKJV	Blessed is the man who trusts in You	Blessed
86:2	NKJV/CEV	Save Your servant who trusts in You	Preserves life, salvation
91:2	NKJV/CEV	My God, in Him I will trust	Fortress, place of safety
105:4	CEV	Trust the LORD	His power

106:24	CEV	They would not trust You, LORD	Were not satisfied in land
112:7	NKJV/CEV	His heart is steadfast, trusting in the LORD	Steadfastness, no fear
115:9	NKJV/CEV	O Israel trust in the LORD	Help and shield
115:10	NKJV/CEV	O house of Aaron trust in the LORD	Help and shield
115:11	NKJV/CEV	You who fear the LORD, trust in the LORD	Help and shield
118:8	NKJV/CEV	It is better to trust in the LORD	Then confidence in man
118:9	NKJV	It is better to trust in the LORD	Then confidence in princes
119:42	NKJV	For I trust in Your word	Gives answers
119:46	CEV	I trust them (teachings) so much	I tell them to kings
119:66	CEV	I trust Your commandments	Gives wisdom/good sense
119:74	CEV	I trust (hope) in Your word	Your servants will be glad
125:1	NKJV	Those who trust in the LORD	Cannot be moved
130:5	CEV	I trust Your promises	All my heart I am waiting
130:7	CEV	Israel, trust the LORD!	Mercy and salvation
131:3	CEV	People of Israel, you must trust the LORD	Now - forever (command)
143:8	NKJV/CEV	For in You do I trust	Loving kindness, guidance
147:11	CEV	Worship Him and trust (hope) His love	This pleases the LORD

Now that we've looked at the Psalms and what they have to say about trusting in the Lord, I have to mention one of my favorite scriptures. It's been the theme of my life.

Proverbs 3:5-6 (NKJV)
"Trust in the Lord with all your heart and do not lean on your own understanding. In all your ways acknowledge Him and He will direct Your paths."

Waiting on the Lord was all I could do at times. I couldn't rely on myself and my thinking because it brought too many bad choices. My wisdom is limited and self-centered. I had to lean on the Lord constantly and not my own understanding. I realized if I relied on my own understanding I would fall, but if I relied on God and his word, I was stable.

During my devotions and journal writing one morning, I came up with this little reminder to help me trust the Lord:

Total
Reliance
Upon the
Surety of
Truth

It's totally laying yourself at the feet of Jesus, knowing he's the only One who can help you. There were times when it was all I could do to just get out of bed in the morning, let alone trust that God would bring me out of my mess. You may have felt the same way at times. Feelings of fear and uncertainty can overwhelm us if we let them. Personally, I had to tell God, "I don't feel like trusting You right now, but I will trust you for trust's sake." Believe it or not, it helped me get through that moment. God is trustworthy even when we don't feel or believe he is. Trust God for trust's sake, if you can't find any other reason to. God will meet you there.

MY DEFENSE

By Kris Belfils

My heart cries out for You, for You are my God
Show Your mercy to me,
You are My defense

My soul silently waits, come and rescue me
Come quickly my Lord,
You are my defense

How I need You and I trust you
You are my God and my refuge
You have changed me, You uphold me
My hope is in You,
You are my defense

My mind is stayed on You, for You are my God
You alone are my Rock,
You are my defense
My strength comes from You, I am weary and weak
Be my Strong Tower,

You are my defense

Chapter 12

STEP 10: SURVIVING LIFE IN THE MUNDANE
Endurance and the Secret Place

This is where we really live, the everyday mundane life. I've found God is truly in the mundane. There's a gentle joy, a peaceful assurance that God gives in the ordinary if you look for it. Yet, the everyday life is sometimes the hardest thing to live. You might have had thoughts like, "What is the purpose of it?" "Why does life take so long to get here?" Life's journey is in the plain, every day processes.

We can get so focused on the future, or the past, that we miss out on the here and now. This is what happened to me. I was looking so hard for my Promised Land; I didn't see or enjoy the everyday life God gave me. There are little joys, miracles if you will, that come with each new day. It took me some time to see them. It might be something in God's word I would read. It might be one of my children giving me a few more hugs then normal. It might be a sunny day when the forecast said it should rain. It might be an awareness of God's joy in my heart all day. It might be a day without pain.

I knew I had to do something to help maintain my sanity. When I came back from the hospital, I needed something to hold on to for each day. Something that made me want to be alive, something I could use to help maintain me in the ordinary. I found some help in the book of Jeremiah.

Jeremiah was considered the weeping prophet. He spent his entire life warning Judah and Israel of God's judgment that would come if they didn't change their ways. Through his entire life, he never had one convert. There are little tidbits you can find in Jeremiah's life that will help you endure each day, even enjoy each day God gives. I also found help from the book of Psalms and Hebrews. Here is a list of ten things I would read or pray each day during my secret place prayer time.

ENDURANCE FOR EACH DAY
Some insights from Jeremiah's life

1. Greet this day as a day with and for the Lord.
2. Remember today; the Lord is my Great Warrior (Jeremiah 20:11).
3. Read God's word today. It will help sustain you, for God's word is "...a lamp unto my feet and a light unto my path." (Psalm 119:105).
4. I commit myself to the Lord and I affirm that commitment today.
5. Know you're on the winning side today!
6. Lord, please give me Your grace to endure this day; not only endure, but to find joy and Your little surprises in it, for You gave me this day. You brought it to me.
7. Be determined to please God in every situation that comes today.
8. Remember God is a God who always has a plan. He has a plan for your life. He has a plan for this day (Jeremiah 29:11).
9. Today, I trust You Lord with the unseen. Help me to remember, "Faith is the substance of things hoped for and the evidence of things unseen." (Hebrews 11:1)
10. Today, I number or order my day for You, Lord. Teach me to follow You throughout the day.

Remember, nothing can overpower you today because God is always there. You're a new creation. You're fully loved and forgiven. God has a plan for your life. Be determined to do your part to help fulfill that plan, stay close to Him!

ON THE SHELF, BUT NOT FORGOTTEN
I found the Secret Place

A few months after I came home from the hospital, the cards, letters and phone calls stopped. In my head, the thoughts "Out of sight, out of mind," kept going over and over relentlessly. I'd wait for cards to encourage me, but they quickly stopped arriving in the mail. I'd come home after grocery shopping or some errand to see if I had messages on my answering machine. I'd wait for the light to flash on my machine to indicate a message was waiting, but it wouldn't be flashing. I'd check my email for just a word of encouragement from anyone, but there was nothing. It was hard to come to the realization that people forgot about me. I know people go on with their own lives, but there is something to be said for reaching out to others, even if they don't reach back. I was in a place that was hard for me to reach out. Shame filled my heart and to try to rid it from me was difficult. In failure, God always moves closer to us. People distance themselves from failure or failures.

I was looking to anyone and everyone for help and encouragement, instead of God. During this time, I learned to go to the "secret place" of the Lord. The place of loneliness taught me to run into the Master's arms and just be. I became desperate for God. I needed strength only He could give me. I made an area out of part of our bedroom, I called my altar area. Ron respected that area, no matter how messy it would get with my wadded up tissues, books, CD player, CD's, and more tissues. This altar area became my safe refuge, my secret place with God. Often I'd be crying out to God in this place for hours. I'd get up, get the kids to school, and immediately go to my secret place of prayer. Then I would get up and make lunch and lay prostrate on the floor in my altar area again, just to be with the Lord. I'd cry out to Him and tell Him my hurts, aches, passions, and then just wait for Him.

At first, He seemed distant. I knew He was around, but was not as near as I'd like Him to be. After a few times, it was as if He walked up to me and stroked my hair while I was lying on my face. My heart leaped. He was there! At that moment, I cried and cried from deep within me. Every time the Lord comes, I weep. His presence is overwhelming. I need Him so desperately, daily. If I were unable to spend time with the Lord in the morning, a few hours later, I'd get an ache in my heart to want to be with Him. This ache would not go away, but increase and become bigger and stronger. It made me go to my secret place. After being with the Lord, I could go throughout my day in a better mindset. It's best to meet with Jesus first, before meeting with anyone else. God showed me how to be with Him continually. I Thessalonians 5:17 states, "Pray without ceasing,..." The secret place with the Lord is in your heart, every moment of every day. We can talk to God always, and He always listens.

When I'm home, I can cry out to God with all my emotions in my secret place. It allows me to vent and get all my frustrations out. We must remember we have the Lord with us always! The Lord longs to be included in all we go through and everything we do. I used to preach on this, but to really live it and experience it on a constant basis, is a totally different thing. I am thankful for my failure in that it brought me closer to my Savior. I've found my secret place with him. I'm not forgotten. In fact, I'm embraced and loved in this precious place daily. As I gave of myself to God in this secret place, God poured Himself in me. I felt safe and secure. This brought me hope and it took my fear away. One day, as I was enjoying my secret place with the Lord, I wrote the song, "Secret Place."

SECRET PLACE

By Kris Belfils

I need You Lord, I trust In You
Though my eyes may not see, Yet I know, You lead me... yeah

I love You Lord, My hope's in You
I will not be afraid of the dark; You light the way

You know the way that I am
You know my heart
I will remain in the secret place with You... yeah

TIME TAKES TIME

Time takes time. Healing takes time. Often we don't want to wait for either. The word "time" used to be a bad four-letter word to me. I hated to wait. I still do, at times. God's time is usually different than our time, and in my case it was. God wanted me to wait and to heal. It was funny to see God use a sore on my finger to get my attention. I accidentally slammed my middle finger on my left hand in my kitchen cabinet door one day. It was painful and swollen. It took a gouge out of several layers of skin. I could just glance down at it and know by sight that I had a sore on my finger. As time passed, the outer surface healed, but the inside of the finger was still tender for me to bend it. Again, through time, I believe it was several months; the pain on the inside slowly went away. I was able to use my finger and hand properly.

Through the process of my finger healing, God showed me what I was like. When my failure first happened and no healing had taken place, I was a big open wound. I wanted to be better, but the fact was I was wounded and needed healing. After some time in rehabilitation with my denomination, counseling, and my secret place with God, I was feeling better about life and myself in general. By all outward appearances, I was looking better, but God was still healing me deep inside, issues I didn't realize I had. Through more months of prayer and counseling, strength came back emotionally, mentally and spiritually. I felt I was ready to minister again, but God didn't. I was kept from ministering through my denomination and just plain circumstances. During this time I had a dream that I was very sick in the hospital. When the nurse came to take my temperature, it was over two thousand degrees. I remember saying in the dream, "Wow, I must be very sick!" Then I woke up. It was a realization that I was sick. God had me in His hospital and He was my Great Physician, constantly taking care of me, watching my healing, every step of the way. Through more time, my finger has totally healed. There is a small scar left, but the finger is healed. There will be scars left from our mistakes. But, through time, God will help you heal, just as He has with me.

The time came for me to minister again by leading worship. Was I ready? I was expecting to have to wait even longer. When the day came for me to step on the platform of the church, get my guitar and start the service, I was apprehensive. In the past, I had led worship so many times; I never gave it a second thought. Now, I was feeling broken, unworthy, and a little scared. I had to rely on God and His strength to minister again. I led worship and the service went well, but I'll never forget that day. God had done such an extreme makeover in me; I felt different and led worship differently. God was the center and strength of my worship leading. A new anointing came upon me as I'd never experienced before. I even had someone prophesy, at a different time, that with one strum of my guitar, with one note sung, God would break the yoke of bondage. I stood in awe as I watched God's powerful hand do just that in the hearts of people. To be honest, I was waiting for someone to rise up in the service and shout, "How can you have her lead worship; don't you know what she's done?" But living in fear is not where God wants me to live. He wants us all to live a victorious life. Through time, and the day to day process, faith was built in me to trust God even in the face of fear. Because F.E.A.R. is really; False Evidence Appearing Real!

I know God healed the deep issues in my heart. It was my prayer and I was seeing my prayer being answered. I knew the healing was permanent. I knew I would not fall back to my old way of thinking and functioning. I truly believed the old was past and all things were new in my life. I was a new creation with a new beginning in my marriage, family, and ministry. How I thought and what I use to do was no longer apart of me. There was newness about my life. A total demolition of the former structure had taken place. Like the home makeover shows that were on television that is exactly what happened to me. There was a new structure built with a new foundation. I was new inside and out. I also knew that if anyone from my past tried to bring up my mistake there would be no life in it. I was not that former person that they knew. It would be like trying to drive a car into my old driveway and into my old garage. There is a new structure there. The new driveway and garage is in a different location. It would be impossible to drive into the old driveway and garage because it is no longer there. If anyone would try and drive a car back into the old driveway and garage, they would see the change and know it can't be done. This is God's transforming power; He makes all things brand new!

Chapter 13

STEP 11: RECEIVING GOD'S DISCIPLINE
Don't Fight the Correction of God

Discipline! Discipline! Discipline! But, God is a God of love, why would He make us endure a hard thing like discipline? We want to hear about God's love, mercy and grace, not His discipline that corrects and rebukes us. The process of discipline is unique for everyone. God knows our character. He knows what pushes our buttons to force us to look at our self and see who and what we really are and the areas we need to change.

Hebrews 12:11 (Amplified Bible)
"For the time being no discipline brings joy, but seems grievous and painful; but afterwards it yields a peaceable fruit of righteousness to those who have been trained by it [a harvest of fruit which consists in righteousness—in conformity to God's will in purpose, thought, and action, resulting in right living and right standing with God]."

For me, I went through a hard first year of discipline. God required me to do no preaching, teaching, worship leading, not even playing an instrument on a worship team. This was excruciatingly painful, yet I know what I had done was wrong, and there were many things needing to change in me. There is, and always will be, an element of joy in ministry for me. Seeing people transformed by the power of God fuels me. It always brings joy to my heart to see a soul saved, or a person lost in the presence of God while worshiping. I had to let go of my ache and desire for ministry. Today, it's still there, but with the right priorities in place.

My pastor and my denomination supervised me. I had to report on books that were assigned, and turn in assignments to my supervising pastor, who met with me on a regular weekly basis. I was held accountable, for which I'm grateful to this day.

So many times on the news we just hear about a minister's failure, but we never hear how that minister walks after they are exposed. We are quick to cast a judging eye at them, I've done it and I'm sure you have too. After experiencing failure as a minister, I now have more mercy and grace for someone who has made a bad choice. I don't condone what they've done, but do understand the pain they might be experiencing. We all need to give more mercy and grace to people, no matter what they've done. If they are truly repentant, and sorry for what they did, extend the arm of mercy to them. Who knows, you might be in need of it someday yourself.

It was hard to admit I needed help. I met with a counselor on a weekly basis. I thought counseling was only for weak people who were not sure of themselves. Well, I was weak, and I was definitely not sure of myself, but counseling is for anyone who wants to work on areas of their life they want to overcome. It was a treasure to have someone listen to me and not criticize what I had done. My counselor would give me ideas to think about and possibly apply to my life. Sometimes I would walk away from my counseling session and never want to return because of what the counselor addressed. Other times, I would leave and feel peace in my heart over my failure knowing that God was working in me and changing me day by day. I appreciated the counselor I had, and would recommend her to anyone. She really helped me out during a tough time in my life.

The discipline was so great; there were times I would cry out to God for Him to lift it. I even prayed for a "jubilee." A "jubilee" is an Old Testament term or celebration. In the New Compact Bible Dictionary, according to Leviticus 25, every 50th year in Israel was to be announced as a jubilee year. There are three main features of a jubilee year; First, "Liberty was proclaimed to all Israelites who were in bondage to any of their countrymen. (In other words, Hebrews that were enslaved for debt were freed, forgiveness would be granted, and they would not have to pay their debt.) Second, return of ancestral possessions to those who had been compelled to sell them because of poverty. Third, It was a year of rest for the land. No crops planted that year."[38] I was enslaved for a debt. I never received a jubilee from man, but I did receive a jubilee from God. Still, God never lifted His faithful hand of correction. Discipline seemed to pour out into every area of my life. I was even stopped by a police officer who gave me a warning because I didn't have a front license plate on my van. Another officer pointed his finger at me when I almost didn't stop at a stop sign. They were all warnings, and I learned to heed them immediately. You see, you can run from God's correcting hand and decide to live your life on your own terms, but in the long run, you are literally self-destructing. Without God being your Shepherd, Protector, and Deliverer, you will walk down a wrong path, which seems fine at the start. But you will end up wishing you never saw the road in the first place.

When one falls into sin, the sin is not necessarily the issue as much as what brought you to that sin. What were the circumstances leading up to it? There must have been a breakdown somewhere in me to bring me to a place I never wanted to be. I realized sin is wrong, and correction is right. I knew being corrected was a good thing, but it was very painful as I went through it. It was not at all "joyful" as Hebrews 12:11 states.

Being away from people, feeling isolated, was another part of the discipline. It was not through my denomination, but what God allowed. I'm a person who likes to be with people, but there were no people around on a day-to-day basis, as when I was an associate pastor. I was away from people, at home, constantly thinking of what I had done, and full of regrets. I do know now, God wanted the place in me that I would fill with people or ministry. He wanted me to run to Him and not people or ministry for my fulfillment. I used to hold ministry with a tight grip. God wanted me to let go of that grip and focus on Him, my husband, and family, instead of on the church family. God had to jolt me to show me this, and isolation was the only way, the only button that could be pushed to show me this. God's hand of correction was extremely heavy the first six or seven months. It was as if God's big hand was holding me down and I was squirming beneath it. The more I squirmed and complained, the heavier His hand of correction was. If I'd relax and rest in the discipline, I'd feel His hand ease up a little, yet it was still holding me down for me to stay put. I did a study on discipline, chastening, and rebuke and here are some of the scriptures I found to be of help, comfort, and gave me insight into why God disciplines His people.

THE DISCIPLINE OF GOD

1. Deuteronomy 4:36 (Amplified Bible)
"Out of heaven He made you hear His voice, that He might correct, discipline, and admonish you; and on earth He made you see His great fire, and you heard His words out of the midst of the fire."

In heaven or on earth, God brings His correction. He has to bring us through the refining fire, for that is the only way our flesh is consumed. But, just like Shadrach, Meshach, and Abednego went into the fire, Christ was there with them (Daniel 3:12-30). God is with us in the fire. If we really try, we can hear His voice comforting us along the way.

2. Job 26:11 (Amplified Bible)
"The pillars of the heavens tremble and are astonished at His rebuke."

3. Psalm 6:1 -10 (Amplified Bible)
"O Lord, rebuke me not in your anger nor discipline and chasten me in Your hot displeasure. Have mercy on me and be gracious to me, O Lord, for I am weak (faint and withered away); O Lord, heal me, for my bones are troubled. My [inner] self [as well as my body] is also exceedingly disturbed and troubled. But You, O Lord, how long [until You return and speak peace to me]? Return [to my relief], O Lord, deliver my life; save me for the sake of Your steadfast love and mercy. For in death there is no remembrance of You; in Sheol (the place of the dead) who will give You thanks? I am weary with my groaning; all night I soak my pillow with tears, I drench my couch with my weeping. My eye grows dim because of grief; it grows old because of all my enemies. Depart from me, all you workers of iniquity, for the Lord has heard the

voice of my weeping. The Lord has heard my supplication; the Lord receives my prayer. Let all my enemies be ashamed and sorely troubled; let them turn back and be put to shame suddenly."

4. Psalm 38:1 (Amplified Bible)

"O Lord, rebuke me not in Your wrath, neither chasten me in Your hot displeasure."

5. Psalm 39:11 (Amplified Bible)

"When with rebukes You correct and chasten man for sin, You waste his beauty like a moth and what is dear to him consumes away; surely every man is a mere breath. Selah!"

6. Psalm 94:12 (Amplified Bible)

"Blessed (happy, fortunate, to be envied) is the man whom You discipline and instruct, O Lord, and teach out of Your law, that you may give him power to keep himself calm in the days of adversity, until the [inevitable] pit of corruption is dug for the wicked. For the Lord will not cast off nor spurn His people, neither will He abandon His heritage."

7. Psalm 118:15 (Amplified Bible)

"The Lord has chastened me sorely, but He has not given me over to death."

8. Proverbs 3:11-12 (Amplified Bible)

"My son, do not despise or shrink from the chastening of the Lord [His correction by punishment or by subjection to suffering or trial]; neither be weary of or impatient about or loathe or abhor His reproof, for whom the Lord loves He corrects, even as a father corrects the son in whom He delights."

9. Proverbs 15:12 (Amplified Bible)

"A scorner has no love for one who rebukes him; neither will he go to the wise [for counsel]."

10. Proverbs 22:15 (Amplified Bible)

"Foolishness is bound up in the heart of a child, but the rod of discipline will drive it far from him."

11. Proverbs 27:5 (Amplified Bible)
"Open rebuke is better than love that is hidden."

12. II Timothy 1:7 (Amplified Bible
"For God did not give us a spirit of timidity (of cowardice, of craven and cringing and fawning fear), but [He has given us a spirit] of power and of love and of calm and well-balanced mind and discipline and self-control."

There is discipline of the correcting kind, and there is discipline of the consistent kind. We need to be disciplined in a lot of areas of our lives. If we are not, we are out of balance. The above scripture talks about having a well-balanced mind. How do we do that? By meditating on God's word, and practicing what it says. We don't like to hear that we need discipline, but it is the healthiest thing we could have in our lives, next to the forgiveness of our sin. God wants us to be consistent and disciplined in our daily life. Disciplined to not over eat. Disciplined to go to work on a daily basis. Disciplined to not over spend our money. This is balance. If we over spend our money, we will have to pay the consequences of not paying our monthly expenses and our creditors will be calling us. If we over eat, we will have to pay the consequence of gaining weight when we didn't want to. If we neglect to show up to work, we have to pay the consequence of possibly losing our job and income for our family.

13. II Timothy 3:16-17 (Amplified Bible)
"Every scripture is God-breathed (given by His inspiration) and profitable for instruction, for reproof and conviction of sin, for correction of error and discipline in obedience, [and] for training in righteousness (in holy living, in conformity to God's will in thought, purpose, and action), so that the man of God may be complete and proficient, well fitted and thoroughly equipped for every good work."

14. Hebrews 12:5-13 (Amplified Bible)
"And have you [completely] forgotten the divine word of appeal

and encouragement in which you are reasoned with and addressed as sons? My son, do not think lightly or scorn to submit to the correction and discipline of the Lord, nor lose courage and give up and faint when you are reproved or corrected by Him; for the Lord corrects and disciplines everyone whom He loves, and He punishes, even scourges, every son whom He accepts and welcomes to His heart and cherishes. You must submit to and endure [correction] for discipline; God is dealing with you as with sons. For what son is there whom his father does [thus] train and correct and discipline? Now if you are exempt from correction and left without discipline in which all [of God's children] share, then you are illegitimate offspring and not true sons [at all]. Moreover, we have had earthly fathers who disciplined us and we yielded [to them] and respected [them for training us]. Shall we not much more cheerfully submit to the Father of spirits and so [truly] live? For [our earthly fathers] disciplined us for only a short period of time and chastised us as seemed proper and good to them; but He disciplines us for our certain good, that we may become sharers in His own holiness. For the time being no discipline brings joy, but seems grievous and painful; but afterwards it yields a peaceable fruit of righteousness to those who have been trained by it [a harvest of fruit which consists in righteousness-in conformity to God's will in purpose, thought, and action, resulting in right living and right standing with God]. So then, brace up and reinvigorate and set right your slackened and weakened and drooping hands and strengthen your feeble and palsied and tottering knees, and cut through and make firm and plain and smooth, straight paths for your feet [yes, make them safe and upright and happy paths that go in the right direction], so that the lame and halting [limbs] may not be put out of joint, but rather may be cured."

15. Revelation 3:19 (Amplified Bible)

"Those whom I [dearly and tenderly] love, I tell their faults and convict and convince and reprove and chasten [I discipline and instruct them]. So be enthusiastic and in earnest and burning with zeal and repent [changing your mind and attitude.]."

Don't fight if you find yourself in discipline right now. Endure and walk through it to the other side. James 1:2-4 (Amplified Bible) states,

"Consider it wholly joyful, my brethren, whenever you are enveloped in or encounter trials of any sort or fall into various temptations. Be assured and understand that the trial and proving of your faith bring out endurance and steadfastness and patience. But let endurance and steadfastness and patience have full play and do a thorough work, so that you may be [people] perfectly and fully developed [with no defects], lacking in nothing." If you run from discipline, and not pay the price now, you will have to pay the price later on in life. Oh, it might not be correction, but it could be your health or consequences for not submitting to correction. Jeremiah 2:19, Amplified Bible states, "Your own wickedness shall chasten and correct you, and your backslidings and desertion of faith shall reprove you. Know therefore and recognize that this is an evil and bitter thing; [first,] you have forsaken the Lord your God; [second,] you are indifferent to Me and the fear of Me is not in you, says the Lord of hosts." I would rather pay the price now, then later. You'll be a much richer person for it and you'll draw closer to Christ through it. The Lord becomes even sweeter after you embrace His correcting hand. He'll show you sides of His character and strength like you've never seen before. Remember that it is only for a season; you'll come out of it and walk on in Christ.

BUILDING TRUST

One more thing that I believe is connected to discipline is; rebuilding trust. First, it will take time for people to trust you again. I lost any trust my husband, friends and family had in me when I made the bad choices that led to my sin. They want to see consistency again. Don't get upset if those you love are shy in trusting you right away. It is okay for them to feel a lack of trust towards you. You let them down, and you let yourself down as well. It is extremely important to do what you say you will do and be where you say you will be. Words will not be enough, your actions are what is needed. There will be pain when someone expresses his or her lack of trust. I felt I had to prove myself time and again with my supervising pastor and leaders. Falling into sin was wrong. I made many bad choices. Yet I felt I could walk through this part of the healing process knowing it was part of the process, and one-day I would be healed.

I want to share a story of rebuilding trust. My youngest daughter Karissa was about seven years old. I took her and her sister to school in the morning like I usually did. When I came to pick them up from school, my oldest daughter came to the car, but no sign of my youngest. Ten minutes passed and still no Karissa. I called the school with my cell phone and talked to her teacher. She informed me that all the children had left, including Karissa. The teacher had her name paged all over the school. When I walked into the school, I quickly started to call her name, "Karissa! Karissa!" Still, there was no sign of her. I went to the office thinking she might be there after the page, but no Karissa. It was twenty minutes after three by now. As I talked to the office staff, one of their phones rang and a lady stated, "I have Karissa Belfils." They quickly gave me the phone as I was frantically thinking someone had taken her. My heart was racing the entire time. The mother on the other end proceeded to tell me that my daughter walked home with her daughter. I never thought my daughter would do that without asking or telling me. I felt a sense of relief that she was safe, yet I wanted to firmly tell her to never do that again. Eventually she told me she wanted to play with her friend and thought I wouldn't let her so she went home without asking me. My husband and I have a policy with our girls that if they want to play with one of their schoolmates, the parents need to talk together first. Karissa didn't want to wait for that. The next day, I was worried that Karissa would do the same thing. I talked to her and she was frustrated and embarrassed about what she had done. I talked to her about trust and what it means and how to rebuild it. I'm not sure if her seven-year-old mind understood the concept, but she did understand mommy worrying about her and that she could have made a better choice that day.

Just like my seven-year-old daughter needing to rebuild trust with her parents on such a simple thing, we need to rebuild trust with those that we love. Trusting yourself to not fall back to your old patterns of sin is a hard process. You know your self. You know what you've done and how you arrived there. You know what you said to yourself to minimize or justify your bad choice. As I was trying to trust myself again, I found several things that helped me trust who I was in Christ.

I was concerned that I would fall back into temptation. I wanted to know if I was developing a pattern of sin in my life. So, I did research on the word, "pattern," and the basic meaning was that it was a repetitive behavior. My findings made me believe I was not developing a pattern because of the change that had happened in my heart. There is change in your heart as well if you have experienced these steps in this book. The pattern is broken! Again, the old has past and all things are new because of what Christ did on the cross for you and me.

First, in my weakness, God is and will be strong. 2 Corinthians 12:9 says, "And He said to me, 'My grace is sufficient for you, for My strength is made perfect in weakness.' Therefore most gladly I will rather boast in my infirmities, that the power of Christ may rest upon me." Our weaknesses are God's place to shine. Not to continue in sin, but to rest in knowing Christ has overcome it on the cross. Satan knows you tripped over it before, so he will try and present it before you again. I believe this is one of the biggest reasons Christ died on the cross for us. Christ knew we would fail. He knew we would be tempted again and again over a given situation. We can rest in His strength knowing He will be there to provide a way out. We can boast in our weakness because Christ's blood has covered it all. This brings Him glory. Our weakness makes Christ's strength perfect, for without it, He would not be needed. Our weakness put Christ on the cross, and His strength, through our weakness, raised Him from the dead. So, when I'm tempted to sin, I rest in the cross of Christ. This brings Him glory. Should I go ahead and sin all the more because my weakness gives Christ glory? Of course not! It's the "after the fact" I'm talking about. It is after we have sinned, asked forgiveness and walked from it and completely turned the opposite direction that we can stand in the fact that Christ is glorified in our weakness. It is why He came to earth in the first place, to be our savior and redeemer.

Second, in my weakness I can hold fast to God and His word remembering what I've learned. I am a new creation, the old has past away and the new has come. I am no longer that person I use to be. I don't think the same, act the same, and function the same way I use to before I sinned. My priorities have changed and I've paid too high of a price in consequences to ever want to taste it again. Now, knowing what I had to walk through has strengthen me and given me a new perspective on the temptation. It doesn't have the lure like it had before. There is no gratification to the flesh because my flesh has been crucified and my will and control have been given back to God. I am a God pleaser now, not a flesh pleaser. I find pleasure in worshiping God rather than pleasing myself. Sin has a stench that I couldn't smell before, it is called, "burnt flesh." I can see why God receives that type of sacrifice of a broken and contrite heart now.

You can start trusting what God has done in you. You can lean on Christ's strength in your weakness. That is how you will start trusting yourself again. You are actually trusting the Christ that lives within you (Galatians 2:20).

Chapter 14

STEP 12: GOD OF THE SECOND CHANCE

A New Beginning

I recently bought a Veggie Tale movie entitled, "Jonah."[39] It is a story of second chances. As I was watching it with my family, God ministered to me through this simple yet powerful child's video.

Here is a short recap of the story of Jonah (See the book of Jonah). Jonah was a prophet who spoke the word of God to people. God asked him to go to Ninevah and speak His word there. Jonah refused and ran the other way because of what the people in Nenevah were doing.

Ultimately, he was swallowed by a big whale and stayed in the belly of this whale for three days. The whale spit him out and Jonah obeyed God and went to Ninevah to tell them to stop sinning.

The people of Ninevah stopped and were forgiven. Jonah wanted to see justice, and God granted mercy. God was a God of second chances!

God granted a second chance in my life. I'm so thankful for God's mercy and the grace that He gives to us. There are many more examples in the Bible of God giving second chances to people.

Here is a study about Levi and the Levites and how God gave them a second chance and even brought them into ministry.

LEVI

A study of Levi and the Levites

Levi has always interested me. He had a sinful past and yet the tribe of Levites was consecrated and used to perform all the duties of the tabernacle. All priests are Levites, but not all Levites are priests. At least, that's what I was taught in my Old Testament Survey class. How could such a tribe be set apart to do the work of the tabernacle and yet have its founding father be a murderer who shed innocent blood, who was a deceiver, and also disobedient to his father, Jacob? This study will bring out all the details and show how God will use people who have a repentant heart and are obedient to His voice.

JACOB AND ESAU

To understand Levi, we must look at Levi's father, Jacob, in order to fully comprehend Jacob's background and family history. Esau and Jacob were twins. Esau came out of the womb first and Jacob came out next, as his hand took hold of Esau's heel. Rebekah, Esau and Jacob's mother, loved and favored Jacob, and Isaac, Esau and Jacob's father, loved and favored Esau (Genesis 25:28). Both boys came out of Rebekah's womb, yet she loved Jacob more. This really shows if we have favorite children, there will be division and discord, and favoritism may affect the descendants to come. Also, playing favorites will cause undue hurt for those who don't receive the same love as the other sibling.

Esau and Jacob fought from the womb and continued after birth. Esau's name means "hairy", because he was red and hairy like a hairy garment all over (Genesis 25:25, NKJV). Jacob's name means literally; "One who takes the heel." He was named this because when he was born, his hand took hold of Esau's heel (Genesis 25:26, NKJV). In the same passage of the New King James Version, Jacob is footnoted as, "supplanter, or deceitful."[40] Also, in the Amplified Bible, Genesis 32:27 says, "[The Man] asked him, What is your name? And [in shock of realization, whispering] he said, Jacob [supplanter, schemer, trickster, swindler]!"

Maybe you've been labeled. Have you believed a remark from

someone in your past? Possibly one of your parents or another adult has said you'll never amount to anything, or you didn't have beauty or grace. Has anyone treated you poorly because of labels placed on you? If so, it is time to break that stronghold on your life. Be determined that your past or what people said about you, will not determine your future.

The boys grew and Esau was a skillful hunter, and Jacob was a mild man, dwelling in tents. Jacob cooked a stew and bought his birthright from Esau. Esau didn't care about his birthright as much as eating. He hadn't eaten for a while. After selling his birthright for stew, he began to despise his birthright (Genesis 25:29-34 NKJV). Their father, Isaac had not blessed the first born yet.

Isaac was getting very old, and his eyesight was poor. When the day came for Isaac to bless the first born with his rightful birthright, he asked Esau to go in the field and hunt game for him and make him savory food to eat so that Isaac might bless him before he died. Esau went out to do exactly what his father requested. Rebekah was listening and heard all that Isaac spoke to Esau and she told Jacob everything. Rebekah told Jacob to go out to the flock and bring her two choice kid goats, and she would make the savory food for his father. She also took the choicest clothes of her elder son Esau, and put them on Jacob. She placed the skins of the goats on Jacob's hands and neck to make him look and feel hairy. Jacob went out with the food to his father, Isaac, and gave it to him.

Genesis 27:18-29 (NKJV)

"So he went to his father and said, 'My father.' And he said, 'Here I am. Who are you, my son?' Jacob said to his father, I am Esau your first born *(lie)*, I have done just as you told me; please arise, sit and eat of my game, that your soul may bless me. But Isaac said to his son, 'How is it that you have found it so quickly, my son?' And he said, 'Because the LORD your God brought it to me *(lie and deceit)*.' Then Isaac said to Jacob, 'Please come near, that I may feel you, my son, whether you are really my son Esau or not.' So Jacob went near to Isaac his father, and he felt him and said, 'The voice is Jacob's voice, but the hands are the hands of Esau.' And he did not recognize him, because his hands were hairy like his brother Esau's hands; so he blessed him. Then he said, 'Are you really my son Esau?' He said, 'I am *(lie)*.' He said,

'Bring it near to me, and I will eat of my son's game, so that my soul may bless you.' So he brought it near to him, and he ate; and he brought him wine, and he drank. Then his father Isaac said to him, 'Come near now and kiss me, my son.' And he came near and kissed him; and he smelled the smell of his clothing, and blessed him and said; 'Surely, the smell of my son is like the smell of a field which the LORD has blessed *(silence is sin if you are trying to deceive)*. Therefore may God give you of the dew of heaven, of the fatness of the earth, and plenty of grain and wine. Let peoples serve you, and nations bow down to you, be master over your brethren, and let your mother's sons bow down to you. Cursed be everyone who curses you. And blessed be those who bless you!"

I added several statements in brackets and Italics to show you all the areas of deception and lies. There were so many lies and deception from Jacob and his mother. Lie after lie and stealing of something that was not promised to him. Esau came in to give his father what he requested and found out Jacob had already been there and stole the blessing from him. This made Esau hate Jacob. Isaac had not passed away yet, but Esau said, "The days of mourning for my father are at hand; then I will kill my brother Jacob." (Genesis 27:41 NKJV) Rebekah found out what Esau said and told Jacob to, "Flee to her brother Laban in Haran. Stay with him a few days, until your brother's fury turns away from you and he forgets what you have done to him; then I will send and bring you from there. Why should I be bereaved also of you both in one day?" (Genesis 27:43-45 NKJV) Rebekah went to Isaac and said; "I am weary of my life because of the daughters of Heth; if Jacob takes a wife of the daughters of Heth, like these who are the daughters of the land, what good will my life be to me?" (Genesis 27:46 NKJV) Another way of manipulating her husband to have it be his idea to send Jacob to Laban's house.

Did you ever watch the movie, "My Big Fat Greek Wedding?" At one point in the movie the daughter wants to help her mother's aunt with her travel agency instead of working at her father's Greek restaurant. The mother, aunt, and daughter come up with the idea of making it be the father's idea to send her to help her aunt. This manipulation has occurred from generation to generation.

The price Rebekah had to pay for this deception was extreme. She lost the love of her son Esau, the son she did love was sent away for years and years and she never enjoyed her grandchildren from him. Actually, Rebekah was never mentioned again. The Bible never mentions when she died or where she was buried. Before Jacob left, Isaac called Jacob and blessed him. This is a double blessing now.

Genesis 28:3-4 (NKJV)

"May God Almighty bless you, and make you fruitful and multiply you, that you may be an assembly of peoples; and give you the blessing of Abraham, to you and your descendants with you, that you may inherit the land in which you are a stranger, which God gave to Abraham."

Before Jacob arrives at Laban's home, he spent the night in Luz, also known as Bethel. During the night, God spoke to him in a dream. God would give to him and to his descendants the land on which he was lying. Also, his descendants would be as the "dust of the earth" and he and his descendants would be blessed (Genesis 28:14 NKJV). This is amazing that God would honor the blessing even though it was obtained through deceit and lies. God is a God of His word and He can see the good in us even in the midst of our sin. Jacob called that place "Bethel" or "house of God" (Genesis 28:17 & 19, NKJV) because God was there and it was the gate of heaven to Jacob.

Genesis 28:20-22 (NKJV)

"Jacob made a vow, saying, If God will be with me, and keep me in this way that I am going, and give me bread to eat and clothing to put on, so that I come back to my father's house in peace, then the LORD shall be my God. And this stone which I have set as a pillar shall be God's house, and of all that You give me I will surely give a tenth to You."

JACOB, RACHEL, AND LEAH

Jacob went on his journey and came to the land of the people of the East. He met Rachel at a well as she was attending her father's sheep. It was love at first sight for Jacob because she was beautiful. Jacob kissed her and told her he was her father's relative and Rebekah's son.

Genesis 29:13-14 (NKJV)

"Then it came to pass, when Laban heard the report about Jacob, his sister's son, that he ran to meet him, and embraced him and kissed him, and brought him to his house. So he told Laban all these things. Laban said to him, 'Surely you are my bone and my flesh.' And he stayed with him for a month. Laban welcomed Jacob to his home and wanted to pay him for his help."

Jacob said he'd work for Laban for seven years and then he'd like to have Rachel for his wife. Laban had two daughters; Leah, whose eyes were delicate or weak, and Rachel who was beautiful of form and appearance (Genesis 29:16-17, NKJV). Laban agreed to Jacob's request. After the seven years were up, Jacob asked for Rachel as his wife. The seven years seemed only a few days to him because of the love he had for her. Later that evening, Laban had a feast. He took Leah, his oldest daughter, and brought her to Jacob, and Jacob lay with her. In the morning, Jacob found out it was Leah. Jacob went to Laban and asked why he deceived him. Now, all the deceiving that Jacob did was happening to him. Laban answered Jacob.

Genesis 29:26-27 (NKJV)

"It must not be done so in our country, to give the younger before the firstborn. Fulfill her week, and we will give you this one also for the service which you will serve with me still another seven years."

Jacob fulfilled the week for Leah. Rachel was given to Jacob, and Jacob fulfilled the seven more years that Laban wanted. Jacob loved Rachel far more than he loved Leah. When the Lord saw that Leah was unloved, He opened her womb and she conceived and bore a son. She called his name Reuben, which means, "see a son,"[41] for she said, "The LORD has surely looked on my affliction. Now therefore, my husband will love me" (Genesis 29:32, NKJV). Then Leah conceived again and bore a son, and named him Simeon, which means "heard,"[42] and said, "Because the LORD has heard that I am unloved, He has therefore given me this son also" (Genesis 29:33, NKJV). She conceived again and bore another son, and named him Levi, which means "attached,"[43] and said, "Now this time my husband will become attached to me, because I have borne him three sons" (Genesis 29:34, NKJV). And she conceived again and bore another son Judah, which means, "praise,"[44] and said, "Now I will praise the LORD" (Genesis 29:35, NKJV). One should note that Jesus Christ came from the tribe of Judah (See Matthew 1:2). There were a total of six sons; Reuben, Simeon, Levi, Judah, Issachar, and Zebulun, and one daughter, Dinah. I could go on and discuss Rachel and her children, but that would be another book. Let's focus on Dinah, Levi, and Simeon.

DINAH

It is best to read Genesis 34 in one sitting before continuing. This will give you more continuity; here we will look at segments of verses to see the sin Levi committed.

Genesis 34:1 (NKJV)
"Now Dinah (which literally means 'judgment'[45]) the daughter of Leah, whom she had borne to Jacob, went out to see the daughters of the land."

There are many speculations to why Dinah "went out to see the daughters of the land." Girls were free to come and go provided their work was done. We see examples of this in Rebekah, who talked to a stranger at the well (Genesis 24:15-21, NKJV), and the seven daughters of the priests of Midian, who chatted with Moses as they watered their father's flock (Exodus 2:16-22, NKJV). Matthew Henry's Commentary states, "Dinah was the only daughter and was very precious to the family, yet she proves neither a joy nor a credit to them; for those children seldom prove either the best or the happiest that are the most indulged. She was fifteen or sixteen years old. Her vain curiosity exposed her. She went out, perhaps unknown to her father, to see the daughters of the land."[46] Yes she was the only daughter and might have wanted other girl friends, but she was a foreigner to the land. She left her home territory. A daughter in that culture was under the legal dominion of her father until her marriage. Her father made all-important decisions for her, such as whom she should marry. Often the daughter was asked to give her consent to the choice of a groom, and sometimes she was even allowed to state a preference, as in the case of Rebekah (Genesis 24:58 NKJV).

The father approved all vows the daughter made before they became binding (Numbers 36:5-12 NKJV). The daughter was expected to help her mother in the home. At a very early age, she began to learn the various domestic skills she needed to become a good wife and mother herself. By the age of twelve, the daughter had become a homemaker in her own right, and was allowed to marry.

Dinah wanted to see the daughters of the land. She wanted to see how they dressed, how they danced, and what was fashionable to them, but I believe she went out to be seen as well. To have some friends, or to see and be seen, either way, the end result was tragic.

We have to look at our motives and why we do the things we do. God knows already. I believe if we really take a sober look at ourselves, we'll not like some of the motives we may find there. But, by God's grace and our willingness, we can lay our weaknesses at the Lord's feet, and ask Him to help us change to be more like His Son.

If Dinah would have obeyed and stayed home, and not given into her young curiosities, she would have prevented many people from dying, and all the loss and pain of the families would have never happened.

Genesis 34:2-3 (NKJV)

"And when Shechem the son of Hamor the Hivite, prince of the country, saw her, he took her and lay with her, and violated (defiled) her. His soul was strongly attracted (clung) to Dinah the daughter of Jacob, and he loved the young woman and spoke kindly (tenderly) to the young woman."

Shechem was a Hivite who was a descendant of Kenaan (Canaan). We find this tribe occupying the district where the Kenaanites (Canaanite) were in possession at a former period (Genesis 12:6). They were not circumcised or even believed in Jacob's God. What Shechem did was horrible. He violated the only daughter of Jacob. Shechem was a prince of the country, but a slave to his own lusts. Matthew Henry states; "He took Dinah and lay with her; not so much by force as by surprise. Great men think they may do anything, and who is more mischievous than untaught and ungoverned youth."[47]

Verse three starts out with "...his soul was strongly attracted to Dinah..." Dake's Annotated Reference Bible brings out, "the soul is the seat of all emotions, passions, appetites, and desires."[48] It was a hunger inside of Shechem to have Dinah. How often have we run with our passions to some place God didn't want us to run? Here, Shechem's passions were untamed and unleashed. They were selfish, lustful desires that only brought destruction and shame.

Genesis 34:4 (NKJV)
"So Shechem spoke to his father Hamor, saying, 'Get me this young woman as a wife.'"

We don't see Shechem confessing to his father with remorse. Shechem wasn't a Jew and didn't know the procedure for making things right before God. He didn't serve God. One must take note: Shechem did love Dinah and wanted to take her as his wife. This really was the noble thing to do at the time. He tried to make the wrong, right. It was fair and commendable, and made the best of what was bad. He loved her, and he asked his father to make a match for him. This was the culture. Shechem did come to his father before his father found out.

Genesis 34:5 (NKJV)
"And Jacob heard that he had defiled Dinah his daughter. Now his sons were with his livestock in the field; so Jacob held his peace until they came."

For Jacob to wait until his sons came from the field indicates his sons were involved and helped with their father's affairs. This was a family affair, but the father was head of the house and had the final say. To wait for his sons, shows that maybe his sons were too involved with his business affairs. The parent should always be the parent or things will go sour if authority is left to a child.

Genesis 34:6-11 (NKJV)

Then Hamor the father of Shechem went out to Jacob to speak to him. And the sons of Jacob came in from the field when they heard it; and the men were grieved and very angry, because he had done a disgraceful thing in Israel by lying with Jacob's daughter, a thing which ought not to be done. But Hamor spoke with them saying, "The soul of my son Shechem longs for your daughter. Please give her to him as a wife. And make marriages with us; give your daughters to us, and take our daughters to yourselves. So you shall dwell with us, and the land shall be before you. Dwell and trade in it, and acquire possessions for yourselves in it. Then Shechem said to her father and her brothers, 'Let me find favor in your eyes, and whatever you say to me I will give.

Shechem was present when his father came to Jacob. If it were a true "rape and run," he wouldn't have shown himself to the family. His actions in this case were honorable, especially for not having God in his life. "Shechem may have been a victim of love at first sight, but his actions were impulsive and evil."[49] He did violate her when he raped her. Not only did he sin against Dinah, he sinned against Dinah's entire family. Soon, the consequences of his actions would be severe both for his family and for Jacob's. Even Shechem's declared love to Dinah couldn't excuse the evil he did by raping her.

I want to stop for a moment and bring a point home. If you're being tempted in a sexual sin, there are many ways to prevent that sin from happening. Don't allow sexual passion to boil over into evil actions. Passion must be controlled. How do we do that? By not constantly thinking and dwelling on doing it. The more you think about it, the more likely you'll do it. God has given us tools, or "weapons," if you will, to use against the enemy's temptations.

TOOLS/WEAPONS TO USE AGAINST LUSTFUL SIN

1. Quote the word of God right back at the enemy, just like Jesus did (Matthew 4).

2. Bring it before God in prayer, and ask forgiveness for even thinking about doing it in your mind.

Matthew 5:28 (NKJV)

"But I say to you that whoever looks at a woman to lust for her has already committed adultery with her in his heart."

3. Pray for strength in your weakness. You are weak in this area or you would not be tempted. Satan knows the right temptation buttons to push in your life. We all need strength when being tempted.

4. Flee from anyone and everything that's connected with the possible sin.

Sin has a lure all its own. There is pleasure in sin or we wouldn't be tempted to do it. Treat sin as a terrible, horrible stench, for it is to God. There are many more ways to flee temptation, but the bottom line is your will. Are you willing to flee? Again, the more you think about that person and being with that person, you will eventually follow through with your thoughts, and the temptation will grow into a full-fledged sin. Stop it before it happens! Set yourself up for success instead of failure. Have someone else in the room, if you have to be with them or make sure you're in a public place. Try, above all, to not be alone with them. If you think you're stronger than the temptation, you're deceiving yourself. The Devil knows your weaknesses, and that's why he's tempting you in this area. You have to soberly look at the temptation and say to yourself, "I might fall if I don't do something!" No one is perfect. Thinking you are above the temptation is a false security. After you sin, there's immediate bondage and you're now a slave to sin. The pleasure you first experienced has gone, and taking its place is shame, guilt, and separation from God. Sin is not worth the cost.

Now let's continue with what happened to Shechem…

Genesis 34:11-12 (NKJV)

"Then Shechem said to her father and her brothers, 'Let me find favor in your eyes, and whatever you say to me I will give. Ask me ever so much dowry and gift, and I will give according to what you say to me; but give me the young woman as a wife.'"

It was the custom to pay a bride price to the father for his daughter's hand in marriage. Sometimes it was money, other times it could be a piece of property or some labor, as in the case of Jacob and Laban.

Genesis 34:13-17 (NKJV)

"But the sons of Jacob answered Shechem and Hamor his father, and spoke deceitfully, because he had defiled Dinah their sister. And they said to them, 'We cannot do this thing, to give our sister to one who is uncircumcised, for that would be a reproach to us. But on this condition we will consent to you: If you will become as we are, if every male of you is circumcised, then we will give our daughters to you, and we will take your daughters to us; and we will dwell with you, and we will become one people. But if you will not heed us and be circumcised, then we will take our daughter and be gone.'"

Hamor and Shechem went back to their people and they did exactly what the brothers asked. The scripture says in verse 19, "….the young man (Shechem) did not delay to do the thing, because he delighted in Jacob's daughter. He was more honorable than all the household of his father." It's interesting that the king and the prince had the men of their city do the same. I'm sure the men of the city were just obeying orders from their king. This is a prime example of people having influence on other people. In this case, Hamor and Shechem influenced their people to follow and all the men of the city did just that. If you're a leader, think twice before you ask your congregation to do something. Is it truly what God wants, or is it what you want? Is it birthed from the flesh or the spirit?

Genesis 34:25-29 (NKJV)

"Now it came to pass on the third day, when they were in pain, that two of the sons of Jacob, Simeon and Levi, Dinah's brothers, each took his sword and came boldly upon the city and killed all the males. And they killed Hamor and Shechem his son with the edge of the sword, and took Dinah from Shechem's house, and went out. The sons of Jacob came upon the slain, and plundered the city, because their sister had been defiled. They took their sheep, their oxen, and their donkeys, what was in the city and what was in the field, and all their wealth. All their little ones and their wives they took captive; and they plundered even all that was in the houses."

We can see Levi and Simeon worked together. They were alike in many ways. They did everything together. They played together, stayed together, ran together, and even killed together. When they were angry, they were angry together. When they were self-willed, they were self-willed together. They even deceived together and received a curse together from their father.

Genesis 49:5-7 (NKJV)
"Simeon and Levi are brothers; instruments of cruelty are in their dwelling place. Let not my soul enter their council; let not my honor be united to their assembly; for in their anger they slew a man, and in their self-will they hamstrung an ox. Cursed be their anger, for it is fierce; and their wrath, for it is cruel! I will divide them in Jacob and scatter them in Israel."

Notice Jacob didn't curse them, but their sin. Remember that there are always consequences to sin. In this case, Levi and Simeon were given a curse instead of a blessing from Jacob. Sons waited all their lives to receive a blessing from their father. But, Jacob never forgot it. I'm sure there was a separation between Levi and Simeon and their relationship with their father. Their sin affected thousands of people. How would you like the world to know your sin from generation to generation?

An interesting thing to know is that later in history, Moses didn't curse the tribe of Levi but gave them a blessing. How could Levi get a blessing after what had happened earlier? Here is the blessing from Moses...

Deuteronomy 33:8-11 (NKJV)
"And of Levi he said: Let Your Thummin (perfections) and Your Urim (lights) be with Your holy one, whom You tested at Massah, and with whom You contended at the waters of Meribah, who says of his father and mother, I have not seen them; Nor did he acknowledge his brothers, or know his own children; for they have observed Your word

and kept Your covenant. They shall teach Jacob Your judgments, and Israel Your law. They shall put incense before You, and a whole burnt sacrifice on Your altar, Bless his substance LORD, and accept the work of his hands; strike the loins of those who rise against him, and of those who hate him, that they rise not again."

Why do I bring all this up? This is the climax of this whole study of Levi! Levi was born into a family of sinners. His father Jacob was a deceiver. Levi and Simeon followed in their father's footsteps. Levi and Simeon did wrong. They deceived, lied, went against their father's wishes, and still God used them. Levi's descendants, the Levites, would eventually take care of the Tabernacle. The book of Leviticus describes their ministry. How can God use someone who wasn't pure? How could God use someone who sinned in such a horrible way?

Levi's name literally means "Joined, adhesion,[50] or attached."[51] But God saw more. Levi and Simeon stood out from their brothers in this terrible act. Their other brothers were not as innocent as it seemed because they helped with collecting the wealth; they had a part in this, too.

Genesis 34:13-14a (NKJV)
"But the sons of Jacob answered Shechem and Hamor his father, and spoke deceitfully, because he had defiled Dinah their sister. And they said to them..."

Genesis 34:27-29 (NKJV)
"The sons of Jacob came upon the slain, and plundered the city, because their sister had been defiled. They took their sheep, their oxen, and their donkeys, what was in the city and what was in the field, and all their wealth. All their little ones and their wives they took captive; and they plundered even all that was in the houses."

All the brothers, I'm sure, had to help and carry all they took home. Still Levi and Simeon were set apart from their brothers by Jacob, Genesis 34:30 (NKJV). "Then Jacob said to Simeon and Levi, You have troubled me by making me obnoxious among the inhabitants of the land, among the Canaanites and the Perizzites; and since I am few in number, they will gather themselves together against me and kill me. I shall be destroyed, and my household and I."

They stood alone among their brothers. At this time, this was a weakness in Levi and Simeon, but God would make it strength. Their character hadn't been refined yet, and this "stand alone" character trait brought a curse from their father.

But, God has a way of taking our weaknesses and turning them around to make them our strengths. With Levi, God saw his unique spirit as a valuable instrument if used the right way. God created Levi, and knew everything about him.

SECOND CHANCES

Let's take a leap forward into history where the Israelites are wandering in the wilderness. Moses was up talking with God on the mountain after he'd just received the Ten Commandments (Exodus 32). Moses had been gone a long time, and the people were getting restless. Aaron was in charge and the people came to him and asked him a question.

Exodus 32:1b (NKJV)
"Come, make us gods that shall go before us; for as for this Moses, the man who brought us up out of the land of Egypt, we do not know what has become of him."

Aaron, who was from the tribe of Levi, and who was Moses' brother, told the people to break off the golden earrings in the ears of their wives, their sons, and their daughters, and bring them to him. Aaron fashioned it into a golden calf and presented it to the people. God wasn't pleased with this and told Moses on the mountaintop that He was going to destroy the people. Moses pleaded with God to not destroy the Israelites. God relented, and Moses came down from the mountain and saw what the Israelites were doing. In his anger, he threw the tablets of the Ten Commandments down at the foot of the mountain. He took the calf, which they'd made, and burned it in the fire and ground it to powder; then scattered it on the water and made the children of Israel drink it. At this point, Moses confronted Aaron.

Exodus 32:21 (NKJV)

"What did this people do to you that you have brought so great a sin upon them?"

Aaron passed the buck and expressed that the people came to him. Aaron asked for their gold and out from the fire a golden calf appeared. When Moses saw that the people were not restrained or naked to other nations because Aaron didn't do his job, Moses stood in the entrance of the camp, and said, "Whoever is on the LORD'S side—come to me! And all the sons of Levi gathered themselves together to him."(Exodus 32:26, NKJV) No other tribe came forward. The Levites stood alone again, but this time, it was the right thing to do. Moses said to them, "Thus says the LORD God of Israel: Let every man put his sword on his side, and go in and out from entrance to entrance throughout the camp, and let every man kill his brother, every man his companion, and every man his neighbor." The sons of Levi did as Moses instructed and about 3,000 men fell that day. I'm sure the Levites didn't know they would have to kill other Israelites that day when they stood alone.

Exodus 32:28 (NKJV)

"Then Moses said; consecrate yourselves today to the LORD, that He may bestow on you a blessing this day, for every man has opposed his son and his brother."

The Levites stood with God. They were consecrated, or set apart for a blessing, and ultimately used for God's service in the Tabernacle. Set apart, isolated! This brought blessing, but I'm sure it was a hard thing to do. They didn't succumb to peer pressure. They stood alone. "The true Levites," says Dr. C. H. Waller, "are the men who have been made lonely among their brethren that they may live alone with Jehovah, and so dwell as the families of others that they may unite them to the family of God."[52] Standing alone was part of the Levite tribe's character. It originated with their founding father, Levi. Now, this act of standing alone was a form of repentance. Their former sin was erased and they were set apart to minister and were used by God. The Levites didn't receive land in the Promised Land, but were able to live in cities. The offerings and tithes were brought to the sanctuary and the Levites were to take their portion of it and live on it. God took care of them.

God is a God of turning things around and making things beautiful again. He's a God of the second chance! Trust Him to do it in your life. He's not interested in our gifts and talents, but in our heart condition. Where's your heart? If you've failed in ministry, allow God to cleanse you, heal you, and transform you into what He wants you to be. The very thing that was your weakness, God can turn into your strength. Be willing to stand-alone with Him. Allow God to take your weaknesses and make strengths for His glory. It's a matter of trust. Trust that God can and will do it. Trust Him when He calls you to be alone or isolated with Him. Trust God in spite of your circumstances. He'll make a way where there seems to be no way. He can turn you and your situation around and make strengths out of your weaknesses.

My Rock and My Song

By Kris Belfils

I breath in You,
I drink in You
Whenever I am lonely, You are there
Whenever I am anxious, all my cares
I give to You, Lord, I give to You

You are my Rock and my Song
The works of Your hands I will sing
You rescued me from my enemies
You are my Rock and my Song

I live in You,
I cling to You
Forever all Your mercies will endure
Forever all my triumphs and failures
I give to You, Lord, I give to You

Chapter 15

I SAVED YOUR TRICYCLE
A Father and Daughter Reunited

During the course of writing this book, God brought something so profound and life changing to my life, I felt I had to add it. It shows how much God loves us and to what extent He will go to bring healing and restoration to His children.

As you read in chapter seven, "Past Effects of Present," my mom and dad were divorced when I was two years old. Throughout the years, I've had maybe four or five phone conversations with my dad, and have seen him twice; once at his mother's funeral and once at my sister's wedding. The last time I talked with him was when my mom died in 1995. We really had no relationship with each other. In fact, I was angry with my dad for not making or keeping contact. We were told by our mom that dad had an affair. My mom planned, and succeeded, in leaving him without letting him know. She left so abruptly that all of our clothes and toys were left in California. Mom never really talked about what happened or why she felt he was having an affair. It was kind of a "taboo" subject. As far as I knew, dad never even tried to come after us.

My dad remarried and so did my mom. Life went on. I would find out little information about my dad through my uncle, dad's brother. Some of the things my dad went through were; a broken back (falling off a two story building), automobile accidents that left him with a metal pipe in his right upper leg, and several strokes that have affected his right side of his body.

Recently, the lady that my dad married passed away. I felt bad for the passing of his wife, but really didn't care about what happened to him. One day in prayer, God brought my dad's name to my mind. I hadn't thought of him in a long time. I felt God was impressing on my heart to take care of my dad. I fought it. I thought, "Why should I take care of someone who didn't take care of me?" But, I've learned not to fight with the Holy Spirit, and eventually I said I would take care of him. I called my dad on the phone, and he was shocked to hear from me. During the conversation I asked him if he wanted to come up to Washington and live with me. He said he was fine, and I left it at that. About a week and a half later, I received a phone call from him telling me that he would like to move and be with me. Now, I was shocked! God asked me to do it, and I had to obey. An overwhelming love and compassion for my dad came over me. I hurried to find an apartment for him so it would be ready for him when he arrived. I drove down to California in order to pack all I could for him. When I arrived at his apartment in California, I walked through the door and saw him lying on his couch. He was worse then I was told. He looked like an eighty-year-old man even though he was sixty-five. He couldn't walk to me, so I ran to him and we embraced and cried. The last time I saw my dad it was at my sister's wedding, more than 20 years ago. He was strong and healthy then.

The drive back from California was an eye opener for me. Dad didn't know why mom had left so quickly. I told him what she had told me, and immediately he denied it. At this point, I told him, "Dad, if you did or didn't have an affair, I would've still come to get you." He was a broken man. He cried. I think we both cried all the way back to Washington. He said he drove up to Washington right after mom left him to find out what happened. He tried to talk to her, he said, but she wouldn't talk to him. So, he went back to California because that was where his job was. I think he felt rejected and thought he didn't have a chance.

Dad would tell me stories of when my sister and I were little girls. I was all ears. He would take us to the store, let us take anything we wanted off the shelves, and he would buy it. When he came home from work, he eagerly waited to see us and would play with us. He couldn't wait to spend time with us. He bought us pretty dresses and toys just because he loved us. He would tell me how cute I was when I was a baby and how I grew to be a beautiful woman. Constantly on our drive home he would tell me how pretty I was. Throughout my life I never thought I was pretty. Ron, my husband, would tell me this, but I didn't believe him. Hearing it from my dad though, really affected me.

At one point, dad looked at me, as I was driving, and said, "You know, I saved your tricycle. It's been in storage all these years." I couldn't believe it. Dad kept my tricycle for almost 40 years? That touched me deeply. After all these years, he still had my tricycle. "I was waiting for you to come home, and wanted you to have it when you did." He said, "I never touched your room or the clothes in it. I left it just the way it was."

Eventually, when he moved away from the apartment we had all stayed in, he put it all in storage. He told me this with tears streaming down his face. I could see he meant it. I could see the tricycle was important to him.

After arriving in Washington State, Dad lived in his own apartment for a few months, but was diagnosed with terminal lung cancer shortly after settling into his new place. At the time his doctor gave him less then six months to live. We cherished the time we had together. We would see each other several times a week. Every time I saw him, he would say his heart jumps, and he could not believe we were together. We both felt like we were kept apart all these years, and couldn't believe we were finally together.

Having my dad back in my life brought so much healing in me. I didn't realize the void I had without my dad. I always felt like something was wrong with me and therefore people didn't like me. I'm sure it stemmed from my thinking that dad didn't come after us or want anything to do with my sister and I. The truth about my childhood has brought closure to unanswered questions. The question of my dad having an affair haunted me all my life. Did he really have an affair? If he did, did he want to be with that person more than being with his two daughters? How can a father not have contact with his children for so many years? I have to say that my failure, and the steps I went through after it, brought a softening in my heart for my dad. If he did or didn't have an affair, it didn't matter. Everyone needs mercy and grace. That is why I went and brought him from California. He was a broken man, full of many regrets.

I wanted to know if Dad believed in God and if he asked Christ in his heart as Lord and Savior. During one of our drives to the doctor, I asked him, "Dad, have you ever asked Christ in your heart as Lord and Savior? He promptly said, "Twice! One time I was even baptized in the river." This brought peace in my heart to know he did have a relationship with the Lord at one point in his life, but I felt God brought him to be with me to help him turn his gaze back onto Him.

My Dad lived in his own apartment for three months. He was very disabled and could hardly take care of himself. I had to make a decision to move him into an adult family home. He was only there for a month and a half before he passed away. I was expecting him to live several more months. Our time together lasted only four months. I'm thankful we had it and a chance for closure. Much healing took place in both of us. Only God could have arranged such a timely reunion.

THE FATHER'S LOVE

Thinking about my earthly father, and how he felt about me, I can't help but think about our heavenly Father and how he feels about us. Just like my dad, God always remembers us. When we turn away from Him, He constantly loves and waits for us to come back. My dad told me about the many times he tried to come up from California to visit me, but was stopped because of some unexpected challenge. A car accident, or needing to bail out a stepchild from jail. Dad said that he bought an old muscle car for me and was going to drive it up and deliver it in person. He soon found out one of his stepsons was in jail, so he sold the car to get him out. Hearing how my dad lived and the choices he made makes me thankful for my mom and how I was raised. My dad lived a hard life. God spared me from it.

God constantly wants to be with us; so much so, He gave the life of His only Son so that we could spend eternity with Him.

If you have turned away from God, He still loves you. He is constantly longing for you to come back. If you feel like you can't come back because of what you might have done, His arms are wide open, and will take you just the way you are. He loves you. He's waiting for you. He kept your tricycle!

Chapter 16

THE GARBAGE MAN ALWAYS COMES ON FRIDAYS

A New Beginning

I found myself being tempted by Satan. I thought I could handle it on my own. Surely, I couldn't tell anyone about it or they would think less of me as a person. After all, I was an approval addict. I craved the approval of others to feel that I was worth something. I performed for results and if I didn't get the results I was hoping for, I'd spiral down emotional and spiritually. When I found myself in sin, I didn't know what to do--after all, I was a pastor. Who could I go to for help? I've heard the expression, "Physician, heal thyself," and know exactly what it means first hand. I had no one to go to for help.

After days of torment, I went to a close friend. I confided in her and told her everything. She loved me and prayed for me. I felt like I finally had someone to hold me accountable, but the sin was too strong. I couldn't escape, as I wanted. I struggled emotionally for two months. I went back to my friend and asked her to help me get out of the slippery pit I was in. She took me to a prayer group out of town, and there, I confessed my sin to God and the group. I went away feeling cleansed and forgiven. I confessed to my husband, my senior pastor, and my congregation, and asked them all for their forgiveness. I thought the church would discipline me "in house" and restore me as associate pastor, but I had to resign. I was devastated.

My world, as I knew it, was crashing down around me and I

couldn't control it.

I confessed to my two young daughters that mommy wasn't a pastor any more because I did something that wasn't all right. Their reaction wasn't what I expected. They understood more then I thought they would. They cried and cried because they didn't want to leave their friends at church. My sin affected so many people and took a huge toll on my own children. I made so many mistakes and knew better, so how was I to walk out of this? Where was I to step first? It seemed too big, too dark! I told myself, "You're a terrible mother, a hypocrite of a pastor, not to mention a sorry excuse for a Christian." How could I change? Within myself, I couldn't, and spiraled down even more into a huge pit of darkness that I so desperately wanted to get out of.

After comforting my children, I told my husband I was going for a drive. I knew all along what I was going to do. I drove for a while and my cell phone rang. It was a pastor friend from another church who'd counseled my husband. He tried to talk to me, but I didn't want to talk. "No one can help me," I thought to myself. My cell phone rang again, and it was my counselor.

"How are you doing, Kris?" she asked.

"I'm doing all right," I lied. All I wanted to do was stop hurting and end my life. I knew the right words to say, so she felt I was fine and ended the call. I bought an iced espresso, then drove to the grocery store to pick up some sleeping pills. "This will do the trick," I thought. After purchasing them, I parked my car off to the side of the store parking lot. It was a hot summer day and I kept the car running to keep the air conditioner on. I swallowed all the sleeping pills with my Iced Mocha Granita. "Now, the hurting will stop!" I whispered. I didn't care about anyone, especially myself. I was angry at the situation, angry at my actions, and angry that I couldn't change a damn thing! I dialed my husband on my cell phone. "Ron, I'm sorry," I cried. He tried to interrupt, but I kept on talking. "I wish I could change everything. I wish I could take away the pain I've caused you!"

"Kris! Where are you?" he yelled.

"I'm not going to tell you," I said.

Realizing I wasn't going to tell him where I was, he tricked me by saying, "I have 911 on my cell phone and you on our home phone. The police are tracing this call and will find out where you are anyway, so tell me!"

"All right. All I will tell you is I'm in a parking lot in Airway Heights," I mumbled, frustrated that I could be found. Couldn't they all see how bad I'd been? Why would anyone want to save me? Can't they see the mess I'd made of my life? I just wanted to be left alone. Alone to sleep and never wake up, and to end this nightmare I was in.

"Let us in!" shouted the police officer outside my window. I was shocked to see police cars in front, behind, and on each side of my van. How did they find me? How did they get to me so fast? I thought.

"Open your door," another officer said firmly. He was standing on the other side of the van, by the passenger window.

"Have I committed a crime?" I mumbled.

"No, we just want to make sure you're all right, so open your door," they demanded.

By this time, the sleeping pills had affected my thinking and speech. I couldn't think straight. I just wanted to sleep, and then all this would go away.

"I'm fine, d-don't worry about me! Please leave me alone." I tried to speak calmly and rationally. Everyone and everything was spinning around me. At that point, the officer at my front passenger window opened the door with a Slim Jim. I heard it unlock and quickly tried to lock the doors with the auto lock button. It worked!

"Let me in!" shouted the officer.

"Will you arrest me if I let you in?" I gasped out.

"No," he answered. He unlocked the door again, and this time, I couldn't stop him. Instead of locking the door with the auto lock, I ended up unlocking all the doors. I was exhausted, and could hardly hold my head up. I was tried of fighting, tired of everything. Now with the doors unlocked, two sets of arms grabbed me, one from my right side and one from my left. They pulled me out of my van and shoved me up against the side of my vehicle and placed handcuffs on my wrists as they were held behind my back.

"I thought you said I wouldn't be arrested! You said I didn't commit a crime!" I yelled.

A kinder officer whispered in my ear, "It's because you resisted letting us in your van, that's why we have to handcuff you."

How did I get to this point in my life?

I looked out past all the vehicles and could barely see my husband walking to our van. How could I face him? Was it too late? Did too much time elapse after taking all the sleeping pills? I was so lonely and life seemed so dark. I truly felt if I were gone, my daughters would have a better life, my husband could move on in his life and people would forget about me. After all, my girls had a dad in their life, which was more than I had growing up. From my vantage-point, I didn't see hope in the situation. How could I move on from where I was? I felt alone and forgotten. But God had His hand on me all the way through this process, and my husband never gave up on me. Thank God for my husband's prayers and unconditional love that he showed continually.

The officers finally took me to the front seat of their police care and took the handcuffs off me. By that time an ambulance had arrived and the paramedics worked on me, giving me IV's and checking my vital signs. They placed me in the ambulance and rushed me to the emergency room.

The next day, I awoke in the hospital and wanted to live, but I didn't know how anymore. I was alive! Somehow, through all this darkness there had to be some light to let me see where to take the next step for living.

We arrived home the following day. "How do I go on from here?' "How do I take the next step forward?" I kept asking myself. All I knew was stripped from me, all but my loving husband and my two beautiful daughters. Then I heard a familiar sound outside our home. A low rumble slowly came down the street to our driveway. It was the garbage man picking up our garbage. *"The garbage man always comes on Fridays!"* I thought to myself. It was a statement that rang like a church bell in my ears. Life does go on and you will too, Kris, one day at a time, one step at a time. I could walk on with my Lord Jesus as I learned to trust Him again. Even if it is trusting God just for trust's sake, I could do it, for He is trustworthy!

The garbage man always comes on Fridays is really a statement of hope. God would eventually teach me to be consistent in my walk with Him, just like the people who pick up our trash are each week. We all have trash that needs to be emptied from our lives. Allow God to clean out all your garbage. It is a weekly, daily, even minute by minute event. Too much trash in our lives will stink up our homes, and too much fleshly garbage in our hearts will do the same. Allow the Master Garbage man to come and pick up all the trash you leave for Him. The key is to leave the garbage out for Him. Search your heart now and ask the Holy Spirit to reveal areas in your life, even your character that needs to be cleaned up. Do you have dirty rags of self-righteousness that need to go? Do you need to change your priorities? What place does God, family, and ministry have in your life? When we allow God access to our "all," God can and will direct us and pour out His blessings as we are faithful and walk in obedience to Him. When we give our all to God, God will be all to us. You can trust him!

BIBLE TRANSLATIONS

1. King James Version (KJV), Published by William Collins + World Publishing Co., Inc., for Riverside Book and Bible House, 1500 Riverside Drive, Iowa Falls, Iowa, 50126

2. New King James Version (NKJV), New King James Version, Broadman & Holman Publishers, Nashville, Tennessee. ©1988. http://www.thomasnelson.com/consumer/dept.asp?dept_id=190660& TopLevel_id=190000

3. Amplified Bible, Zondervan, Grand Rapids, Michigan. ©1954, 1958, 1962, 1964, 1965, 1987 by The Lockman Foundation. ©1987 By Zondervan. http://zondervan.com/desk/rights.asp?Page=permampbib

4. Contemporary English Version (CEV), E-Sword, ©2004, Rick Meyers, (www.e-sword.net)

5. New International Version (NIV), The NIV Study Bible Copyright ©1985 by the Zondervan Corporatoin. http://zondervan.com/desk/rights.asp?Page=permbible

6. The Message, The Bible in Contemporary Language Copyright ©1993 1994, 1995, 1996, 2000, 2001, 2002. By Eugene H. Peterson. All rights reserved. www.e-sword.com Rick Meyers.

ENDNOTES

1. Kristine A. Belfils, ©2002, song "Cross of Grace," from Brokenness CD.

2. Stormie Omartian, The Power of a praying Husband, Harvest House Publishers, ©2001.

3. Stormie Omartian, The Power of a praying Wife, Harvest House Publishers, ©1997.

4. Robert S. McGee, W. Search for significance, Publishing Group, Thomas Nelson Publishers, ©1998.

5. Robert S. McGee, W. Search for significance, Publishing Group, Thomas Nelson Publishers, ©1998.

6. Joyce Meyers, How To Hear The Voice of God, Warner Faith, A division of AOL Time Warner Book Group, ©2003.

7. John C. Maxwell, Falling Forward, Thomas Nelson Publishers, ©2000.

8. Christian Literature Crusade, Fort Washington, PA., Amy Wilson (1867-1951).

9. Exodus 2:24, 3:6, 4:5, 6:3, 33:1, Leviticus 26:42. Numbers 32:11, Deuteronomy 1:8, 6:10, 9:5b, 29:13, 30:20b, 34:4, II Kings 13:23, Matthew 22:32, Mark 12:26, Luke 13:28, (KJV).

10. Genesis 25:26 New King James Version, Holman Bible Publishers, ©1988, Thomas Nelson, Inc. Reference notes from center column.

11. E-Sword, ©2004, Rick Meyers, 2000+ Bible Illustrations.

12. Andrew Murray, A Life of Obedience, ©1982, Bethany House Publishers.

13. Thorndike Barnhart Comprehensive Desk Dictionary, Double Day and Company, Inc. ©1952, 1953, 1954, 1955, 1956, 1957, 1958, 1962, 1965, 1967, by Scott Foresman & Company. Edited by Clarence L. Barnhart.

14. Brown Driver Briggs Hebrew Definitions, E-Sword Bible software, Strong's Hebrew and Greek Dictionary, E-Sword Bible Software version 6.50, ©2004. "Canaanites" Strong's #H3669.

15. Brown Driver Briggs Hebrew Definitions, E-Sword Bible software, Strong's Hebrew and Greek Dictionary, E-Sword Bible Software version 6.50, ©2004. "Kenaan" Strong's #H3667.

16. Brown Driver Briggs Hebrew Definitions, E-Sword Bible software, Strong's Hebrew and Greek Dictionary, E-Sword Bible Software version 6.50, ©2004. "Kana" Strong's #H3665, at this form it is a verb, and is a primitive root.

17. Brown Driver Briggs Hebrew Definitions, E-Sword Bible software, Strong's Hebrew and Greek Dictionary, E-Sword Bible Software version 6.50, ©2004. "Hittite" Strong's #H2850.

18. Brown Driver Briggs Hebrew Definitions, E-Sword Bible software, Strong's Hebrew and Greek Dictionary, E-Sword Bible Software version 6.50, ©2004. "Heth" Strong's #H2845.

19. Brown Driver Briggs Hebrew Definitions, E-Sword Bible software, Strong's Hebrew and Greek Dictionary, E-Sword Bible Software version 6.50, ©2004. "Chathath" Strong's #H2865, at this form it is a verb, and a primitive root.

20. Brown Driver Briggs Hebrew Definitions, E-Sword Bible software, Strong's Hebrew and Greek Dictionary, E-Sword Bible Software version 6.50, ©2004. "Hivittes" Strong's #H2340.

21. Brown Driver Briggs Hebrew Definitions, E-Sword Bible software, Strong's Hebrew and Greek Dictionary, E-Sword Bible Software version 6.50, ©2004. "Chavvah" Strong's #H2333.

22. Brown Driver Briggs Hebrew Definitions, E-Sword Bible software, Strong's Hebrew and Greek Dictionary, E-Sword Bible Software version 6.50, ©2004. "Perizzites" Strong's #H6522, #H6521.

23. Brown Driver Briggs Hebrew Definitions, E-Sword Bible software, Strong's Hebrew and Greek Dictionary, E-Sword Bible Software version 6.50, ©2004. "Peraziy" or "peroziy" Strong's #H6521.

24. Brown Driver Briggs Hebrew Definitions, E-Sword Bible software, Strong's Hebrew and Greek Dictionary, E-Sword Bible Software version 6.50, ©2004. "Perazah" Strong's #H6519.

25. Brown Driver Briggs Hebrew Definitions, E-Sword Bible software, Strong's Hebrew and Greek Dictionary, E-Sword Bible Software version 6.50, ©2004. "Paraz" Strong's #H6518.

26. Brown Driver Briggs Hebrew Definitions, E-Sword Bible software, Strong's Hebrew and Greek Dictionary, E-Sword Bible Software version 6.50, ©2004. "Girashite" or "Girgasite" Strong's#H1622.

27. Brown Driver Briggs Hebrew Definitions, E-Sword Bible software, Strong's Hebrew and Greek Dictionary, E-Sword Bible Software version 6.50, ©2004. "Amorite" Strong's #H567.

28. Brown Driver Briggs Hebrew Definitions, E-Sword Bible software, Strong's Hebrew and Greek Dictionary, E-Sword Bible Software version 6.50, ©2004. "Amar" Strong's #H559, it is a verb and brought to the primitive root.

29. Brown Driver Briggs Hebrew Definitions, E-Sword Bible software, Strong's Hebrew and Greek Dictionary, E-Sword Bible Software version 6.50, ©2004. "Jebusite" Strong's #H2983.

30. Brown Driver Briggs Hebrew Definitions, E-Sword Bible software, Strong's Hebrew and Greek Dictionary, E-Sword Bible Software version 6.50, ©2004. "Jebus" Strong's #H2982.

31. Brown Driver Briggs Hebrew Definitions, E-Sword Bible software, Strong's Hebrew and Greek Dictionary, E-Sword Bible Software version 6.50, ©2004. "bus" Strong's #H947, at this form it is a verb, and brought to the primitive root.

32. Psalm 9:14 KJV footnote, "public presence," Living Word Reference Addition, Riverside ©1976, Thomas Nelson, Inc. Nashville, TN., page 864.

33. Strong's Hebrew & Greek Dictionaries, E-Sword, Rick Meyers, ©2004.

34. Strong's Hebrew & Greek Dictionaries, E-Sword, Rick Meyers, ©2004.

35. Strong's Hebrew & Greek Dictionaries, E-Sword, Rick Meyers, ©2004.

36. The Student Bible Dictionary, Barbour Publishing Group, Inc., Uhrichsville, OH. ©2000 Karen Dockrey, Johnnie Godwin, and Phyllis Godwin, page 76.

37. Rev. Charles H. Spurgeon, (www.spurgeon.org/sermons/0312.htm) towards the end of the sermon; "Personal Service." Delivered on Thursday evening, May 3rd, 1860, at Survey Chapel, Blackfairs road.

38. The New Compact Bible Dictionary, ©1967 by Zondervan Publishing House, Grand Rapids, Michigan, page 297. The Student Bible Dictionary, Holman Bible Publishers, ©1993 and 2000, Barbour Publishing, Inc., Uhrichsville, OH., page 137.

39. Jonah, A Veggietales movie, ©2002, Big Idea Productions, Inc.

40. New King James Version, Broadman & Holman Publishers, Nashville, Tennessee, ©center column note, page 21.

41. New King James Version, Broadman & Holman Publishers, Nashville, Tennessee, ©center column note, page 25.

42. New King James Version, Broadman & Holman Publishers, Nashville, Tennessee, ©center column note, page 25.

43. New King James Version, Broadman & Holman Publishers, Nashville, Tennessee, ©center column note, page 26.

44. New King James Version, Broadman & Holman Publishers, Nashville, Tennessee, ©center column note, page 26.

45. New King James Version, Broadman & Holman Publishers, Nashville, Tennessee, ©center column note, page 26.

46. Matthew Henry's Commentary, Volume 1, Genesis to Esther, Sovereign Grace Publicers of Marshallton, Delaware, U.S.A. Genesis XXXIV, note 1, page 117.

47. Matthew Henry's Commentary, Volume 1, Genesis to Esther, Sovereign Grace Publicers of Marshallton, Delaware, U.S.A. Genesis XXXIV, note 1, page 117.

48. Dake's Annotated Reference Bible, ©1963, 1991. Finis Hennings Dake, Dake Bible Sales, Inc., Lawrenceville, Georgia. Genesis letter "J", page 33.

49. Life Application Bible, New International Version, Notes on Genesis 34:1-4, page 71, Tyndale House Publishers, Inc., Weaton, Illinois and Zondervan Publishing House, Grand Rapids, Michigan, ©1988, 1989, 1990, 1991.

50. All the Men of the bible, Zondervan Books, Zondervan Publishing House, Grand Rapids, Michigan, ©1958, under "Levi," page 217.

51. New King James Version, Broadman & Holman Publishers, Nashville, Tennessee. ©1988, center column note for Genesis 29:34, page 26.

52. All the Men of the bible, Zondervan Books, Zondervan Publishing House, Grand Rapids, Michigan, ©1958, under "Levi," page 218.

12424456R00080

Made in the USA
Charleston, SC
04 May 2012